Belle Gunness:

The True Story of The Slaying Mother

by
Jack Rosewood
&
Rebecca Lo

Historical Serial Killers and Murderers
True Crime by Evil Killers
Volume 14

GET THE BOOK ABOUT HERBERT MULLIN FOR FREE

Go to \underline{\text{www.jackrosewood.com}} www.jackrosewood.com

and get this E-Book for free!

Contents

Introduction

From a poverty-stricken family in a remote village in Norway, to a farm in La Porte, America, surrounded by riches, the story of Belle Gunness will astonish and frighten you. To think that a woman such as this could have lived happily amongst the community, while all the time hiding a horrific secret, is unbelievable.

Belle Gunness was a tall, heavy-set Norwegian woman that most who came to know her found to be personable and friendly. But the true Belle was a woman who carried out multiple murders, fraud and theft, right under the noses of the neighbors. When the truth came out about what Belle had been doing up there at her farmhouse, the people of La Porte would never be the same again.

Men were lured into her clutches through newspaper advertisements, claiming she was wealthy and looking for love. But in actual fact, she wasn't looking for romance at all, she was looking for money. Once she got what she wanted out of them, the many suitors were cast aside with a meat cleaver to the head and buried under the pig pen. Some of them weren't even fortunate enough to be buried, instead being fed to the pigs at night, under the veil of darkness so as not to be discovered.

Of course none of this would have been discovered if it wasn't for a dreadful fire at the farmhouse. In the smoldering ruins were found the body of a woman, minus her head, and the bodies of Belle's three children. Sympathy was initially shared by everyone that had known Belle, or who lived nearby, for the loss of this poor woman and her delightful children. It wasn't until the identification of the headless corpse was questioned, that the wheels were set in motion for a discovery that would shock the country.

After the suspicion of whether or not it was Belle's body in the ruins of the burnt out house arose, Belle would come to be known by other names, such as Lady Bluebeard, the Black Widow of La Porte, and Hell's Belle. She would become a legend, for all the wrong reasons, and children were warned to behave in case Belle showed up and took them away. Big, strong farmers would peer over their shoulder, constantly on the lookout for evil Belle. The people of La Porte would make sure they were home before dusk, in case she was hiding in the shadows.

The biggest question of all surrounding Belle Gunness was not why she murdered so many people. The answer to that was very clear. No, the unsolved mystery that still remains today, was whether Belle died in the fire, or whether she escaped and assumed the identity of another woman, called Esther Carlson, going on to commit other murders later in life.

So many questions, so many mysteries. The story is so abhorrent it is almost as though it is a work of fiction. How could a woman do the things she did and not feel remorse? Women are supposed to be the weaker sex, the emotional humans, yet Belle exhibited none of that. Instead, she tossed the bodies of her victims over her shoulder, carried them down the stairs into the basement, and set about the task of getting rid of them.

The story of Belle Gunness and the crimes she committed is not one for those who are faint of heart. The gruesome murders, the framing of an innocent man, the sacrifice of her own children, and the dismemberment and disposal of the victim's bodies, are the stuff of real nightmares. Never before had a female serial killer matched the coldness and cruelty of Belle Gunness. And hopefully, we will never see another like her again.

CHAPTER 1:
From Norway to America

This disturbing biography of one of America's worst ever serial killers begins not in the United States as one would think, but in a very small village in Norway. Very little is known about the childhood of Belle, though given the nature of the environment she was borne into, it is not difficult to see how it may have affected her throughout her life. Often how we start out in life can greatly affect how we continue through adulthood.

The Beginning of Belle

Belle Gunness was born Brynhild Paulsdatter Størseth on the date of November the 11th, 1859. Her father's name was Paul Pedersen Størseth, who worked as a stonemason, and her mother was Berit Olsdatter. There were eight children in the family, of which Belle was the youngest. The family was very poor, and this led to some bullying, particularly of Belle.

The family lived in a tiny cotter's farm in Innbygda, located in the municipality of Trysil, Norway. This very small village was bleak, with severe winters that resulted in blanketing of heavy snow. The main form of transport was by ski, and subsequently in 1862, the very first organized ski race took place here.

The nature of the weather and the remoteness of Innbygda meant that the nearest living soul was often more than a day's travel away. This isolation could have had a detrimental effect on Belle as a child, and goes a long way towards explaining why she eventually left.

Evidence of Belle's behavior and attitude as a child is very scant, and the descriptions are very different, and are therefore more likely inaccurate. Some had described her as an exemplary child, meaning she was good-natured and well-behaved. However others described Belle as being capricious, malicious, a prolific liar, and would often play unpleasant tricks on people. Which of these descriptions is a true report of Belle as a child remains a mystery.

A Dreadful Affair

A story emerged of an awful event leading to tragedy for Belle in 1877, and although it was never verified officially, if it was true, it could have been the catalyst that triggered what would later become a horrific series of murders.

Allegedly, Belle was pregnant in 1877, at the age of 18. There is no record of who the father of the baby was, which is unusual in such a small village, but that is not the main issue. Whilst attending a dance, a man kicked her in the stomach, and Belle lost the baby. This man was apparently from a very wealthy family, and he was never arrested or charged for the assault.

Interestingly, this man was to die shortly after, supposedly of stomach cancer, but one has to wonder in hindsight if that was the real cause of death. Those who knew Belle at this time claimed that overnight her personality changed, and not for the better.

A Description of Belle

Some reports put Belle at the height of six feet, which would have made her quite an imposing woman. She had the typical Norwegian blonde hair and blue eyes, and was considered rather attractive when she was young. As she got older, she learnt to use her womanly wiles, by using corsets to emphasize her bust, which was an impressive 48 inches. Her figure was that of an hourglass, which was popular in that era, and would have caught the eye of many a man.

The Big Move

A year after the tragic miscarriage, Belle took service with a family on a very large farm, and she continued to work there for three years. During this time, she saved as much money as she could, so she could leave Norway. Her older sister Nellie, had immigrated to America earlier, and so Belle developed a plan to follow her, in search of a better life.

Belle's dream came to fruition, and in 1881, when she was old enough, she moved to America. It was at this time that she assumed the name Belle, as it sounded more American, and she wanted to fit in. She had settled in Chicago, Illinois, and continued to work as a servant for a few years.

Luckily, the community she settled in contained a large number of fellow Norwegians who had also immigrated to America, so she was not without people of her own. This would have helped Belle settle in, as she could talk in her native tongue, and share stories about her day with those that were similar to her. Often the biggest challenge when moving to a different country is the culture shock. The larger populations, the bigger cities, they all would have been astonishing for a poor girl from a tiny village that was isolated and often blanketed in snow.

CHAPTER 2:
Belle Meets a Husband

Belle had met a man in Chicago and she subsequently married him. This would end up being the longest relationship Belle ever had, and they would ultimately be separated by his death. It was during this union, that Belle would have her first experience of gain from insurance.

Mads Sorenson

Mads Ditlev Anton Sorenson was a store guard when Belle met him, and they married in 1884 in Chicago. Two years after they married they set up and opened a confectionery store; however it was not a successful business. Within one year of opening, the store burned down, with Belle claiming it was due to an oil lantern. Despite the fact that no lantern was ever found in the ruins, Mads and Belle received an insurance payout.

The couple purchased another home, and by all reports, their domestic life seemed to be happy. There are differing reports regarding their children, as to whether they were biological or adopted. What is known is that there were initially four children – Axel, Caroline, Myrtle and Lucy. There are also reports of some of these children plus another girl called Jennie (though some believe she was actually Morgan Couch and they changed her name) was adopted from poorer families in the neighbourhood.

The first two children, Axel and Caroline, died whilst still in infancy. Their manner of death was listed as acute colitis, a condition that affects the gastrointestinal system. Both of these children were insured, and the parents received payment after they died. What some researchers have pointed out is that the symptoms of acute colitis are almost identical to the symptoms experienced due to many types of poisonings.

The family continued to have terrible experiences with fire, having to move three times due to their houses burning down. How one family could have such bad luck is virtually impossible, and the fact that they always received insurance payouts should have been a clue as to what was really going on.

The Death of a Husband

On the 29th of July, 1900, Mads was complaining of suffering pains in his chest. He had been undergoing treatment by his doctor for an enlarged heart, so when he passed away the following day, it was naturally assumed he had died of a heart attack. However, the first doctor who assessed him felt that Mads was suffering from strychnine poisoning. Given the previous history of a heart condition, this opinion was ignored, and the cause of death was certified as heart disease, with no autopsy required. Of note, Belle had said that she had been giving Mads some form of medicinal powders to make him feel better, but this was never investigated.

The very day of his death, the 30th of July, was the one and only day when two insurance policies on his life would overlap. The day after Mads died, Belle put in an application for the insurance money on both policies. Because of the speed at which the claim was made, and the coincidence of the timing of the death and the overlapping policies, an inquest was to be ordered. The family of Mads requested his body be exhumed and tested for arsenic, as they also suspected poisoning. Unfortunately though, the inquest and the exhumation never occurred, and Belle was awarded a staggering $8,500, which was a vast sum of money in those days.

Moving To the Farm

With her newfound wealth from the insurance payouts, Belle decided to buy herself a farm. She settled on one located on the outskirts of the town of La Porte, in Indiana, packed up her three surviving children and moved in, in 1901. The house was two-storied and made of red brick, and boasted six bedrooms. On one side of the house was an orchard, with a forest and shallow swamp on the other side.

The farm ran parallel to McClung road, and has once been a house of disrepute, a brothel run by a Madame by the name of Mattie Altie. It reeked of stale perfume, and Belle set about airing out the whole house. With marquetry floors, and dark walnut interiors, the house was quite impressive, and with Belle's touch, it was transformed into a comfortable home for her and her children.

Interestingly, shortly after they moved in to the house, the carriage and boat houses burned to the ground. Had Belle once again resorted to insurance to finance her coffers? Most likely. Belle had spent quite a bit of money in repairing and upgrading the house, including the addition of a six foot fence around the hog pen, complete with barbed wire atop.

CHAPTER 3:
Husband Number 2

Before moving to the farm in La Porte, Belle had met up with a man she had known previously. Having recently lost his wife, Peter Gunness was also born in Norway and immigrated to America. It seemed they had plenty in common.

Married Life

Belle and Peter married in La Porte, on the 1st of April, 1902. The people of La Porte were surprised to see Belle suddenly have a husband in tow. Peter was an attractive man, tall with blonde hair and a beard, and he was an experienced farmer. He brought with him his infant child and older daughter from his previous marriage, and tragically just a week following the wedding ceremony, the child died. It was reported that the child contracted a viral illness whilst alone with Belle.

Despite the loss of his child, Peter set about helping Belle run the farm, along with the assistance of Belle's children. There was much to do to manage the cornfields, and Peter and Belle were often seen in town selling their produce or their cattle.

Life seemed to be moving along well for the new family, but this would not last for long.

The Demise of Peter Gunness

Till death do us part seemed to ring true for Belle's marriages, as it wasn't long before Peter died and she was once again a widow. Peter died in December, 1902, having only married Belle in April of that same year. The story given by Belle was that Peter had been reaching for his slippers when he was scalded with hot brine cooking on the stove. He was then struck on the head by a meat-grinding machine which had fallen off a shelf above the stove.

Jennie had heard the commotion and rushed downstairs to see Peter writhing in pain on the floor, with Belle standing over him. Not deceased straight away, Peter would be dead before the sun came up.

Deathly Suspicions

Once again Belle reaped the financial benefits from the death of a husband. Like her previous husband, Belle had a life insurance policy out on Peter, and when he died, she received an estimated $3,000.

The people of La Porte found the story of Peter's death to be ludicrous, given that he was such an experienced farmer and a fit and healthy man. The suspicions reached the ear of the district coroner, who having reviewed the case, declared that

Peter had been murdered. A coroner's jury was instructed to investigate.

Despite their best intentions, Belle was able to convince the jury that she was completely innocent, and that Peter's death had been nothing more than a tragic accident. Once again she seemed to get away with murder. Peter's brother removed his niece Swanhild, Peter's child by his first wife, from Belle's home a year after his death. This would be crucial, as this child is the only one who survived living with Belle.

At the time of the investigation into Peter's death, Belle was actually pregnant with Peter's child, yet for some reason she did not make that fact known to the jury. In the May of 1903, her son Philip was born. Towards the end of 1906, Belle informed her neighbours that her adopted daughter Jennie had gone away to a finishing school in Los Angeles. It would be some time later that this story would prove to be a lie.

CHAPTER 4:
Advertisement for Love

Following the death of her husband Peter, Belle continued to run the farm on her own with the help of her children. In 1907, she decided to hire a farm hand. During this same time, she was also looking for 'love'.

A Multitude of Suitors

Around 1907 Belle went to the effort of placing an advertisement in the paper to attract men. The advertisement was placed under the matrimonial section of all of the daily newspapers in Chicago and in many other large cities in the Midwest. Her advertisement read as follows:

Personal – comely widow who owns a large farm in one of the finest districts in La Porte County, Indiana, desires to make the acquaintance of a gentleman equally well provided, with view of joining fortunes. No replies by letter considered unless sender is willing to follow answer with personal visit. Triflers need not apply.

This proved incredibly popular and successful, with many middle-aged gentlemen of means responding. One of the first men to apply was John Moe from Minnesota. He arrived at the farm carrying $1,000, and he told the neighbors that he was using it to pay off Belle's mortgage. He was not introduced as a suitor; instead Belle told everyone he was her cousin. John Moe disappeared within a week of arriving at the farm.

They Came but Did They Leave

Many suitors continued to respond to Belle's advertisements, and although they were often seen arriving at the farm, they were never seen leaving. At the same time, Belle ordered many large trunks to be delivered to her farm. Being a tall, strong woman, she carried these effortlessly, and the delivery man would later remark that she seemed to lift and move the trunks as though they were as light as marshmallows. Belle had also become more secretive, keeping the curtains and shutters closed 24 hours a day to keep out prying eyes.

Another suitor who arrived on her doorstep was an elderly man who had been widowed, called Ole B. Budsberg. He had come all the way from Iola, Wisconsin, where he owned land. The last time Budsberg was seen alive, was on the 6th of April. 1907. He had been in the bank where he mortgaged his land back in Wisconsin and signed over a deed. He also withdrew a large amount of cash, several thousand dollars in fact.

His two grown sons did not know that their father had gone to see Belle, and when they found out, they sent her a letter asking of his whereabouts. Belle wrote back to the sons, telling them that she had never seen or met their father.

Throughout 1907, many men came to the farm then disappeared quickly. They were never there for very long, and it seemed as though they had just visited briefly. One such man arrived in December 1907, and was called Andrew Helgelien. A farmer from South Dakota, Helgelien replied to Belle's advertisement in writing, and being a bachelor of means, his approach was warmly greeted by Belle. They began to write letters back and forth, one of which from Belle was found at the Helgelien property at a later date, which read:

"To the Dearest Friend in the World: No woman in the world is happier than I am. I know that you are now to come to me and be my own. I can tell from your letters that you are the man I want. It does not take one long to tell when to like a person, and you I like better than anyone in the world, I know. Think how we will enjoy each other's company. You, the sweetest man in the whole world. We will be all alone with each other. Can you conceive of anything nicer? I think of you constantly. When I hear your name mentioned, and this is when one of the dear children speaks of you, or I hear myself humming it with the words of an old love song, it is beautiful music to my ears.

My heart beats in wild rapture for you, My Andrew, I love you. Come prepared to stay forever."

On receiving this letter, Helgelien didn't hesitate to make his way to Belle's side, arriving in January 1908. He brought a check with him valued at $2,900 which was his savings. Just a few days after his arrival, Helgelien and Belle visited the Savings Bank in La Porte and deposited the check. Although Helgelien disappeared a few days later, Belle continued to make deposits to this account, one for $500 and another for $700.

The Ones That Got Away

Despite such a large number of suitors responding to Belle's advertisement, there were just a few that managed to escape her clutches. One of these was a fellow immigrant from Norway, called George Anderson. Anderson travelled from his home in Missouri to meet with Belle, and whilst they were having dinner together, Belle brought up the subject of her mortgage. Anderson stated that he would pay off her mortgage if the decided they would marry.

Anderson went to bed in the guest room, and during the night he awoke to find Belle standing there staring into his eyes while holding a candle. Anderson was shocked and startled, and later claimed she had such a sinister look on her face that he yelled out, and she fled from the room.

Wasting no time, Anderson quickly got dressed and fled from the house. He took no time to say goodbye, he just felt he needed to leave as quickly as possible. Even as he ran, he constantly looked over his shoulder fully expecting Belle to be chasing after him. Anderson boarded the train back to Missouri and never made contact with Belle again, not even to arrange for his belongings to be sent.

A horse dealer and farmer from Kansas, Lon Townsend was also in correspondence with Belle. She had sent him many letters, asking him to come and visit with her. Townsend had decided not to visit Belle until the following spring, but by then the fire had occurred at the farm, so he never got to meet her.

Another gentleman from Arkansas was corresponding with Belle, but he too did not get time to visit before the fire. The last letter from Belle to this man was sent on the 4th of May, 1908. There was also an allegation that Belle had promised to marry a man called Bert Albert, but she cancelled the arrangement due to his lack of finances.

CHAPTER 5:
The Farmhand

Ray Lamphere was hired by Belle to work as a farmhand in 1907. She needed help to run the farm, but little did Ray know what the consequences of this employment would be.

Ray Lamphere

Ray was willing to do any job or chore that Belle asked of him, as he had fallen in love with her. He watched so many suitors come to the farm to woo Belle, and his jealousy intensified with each new arrival. He started to cause trouble by making scenes, so on the 3rd of February 1908, Belle fired him.

Not long after Ray's firing, Belle went to the La Porte County courthouse, and stated that her former employee, Ray, was not of sound mind, and that he was a menace to the people of La Porte. Based on her claims, a sanity hearing was held to determine the mental status of Ray. He was found to be sane, and was released back into the community. Just a few days later, Belle returned to the sheriff and claimed that Ray had come to the farm and argued with Belle. Subsequently, Ray was arrested for trespassing, and Belle made it known that she felt he was a threat to her and her family.

The Threat of Ray

Each time Ray attempted to visit Belle at the farm she drove him away. He had made a few threats, and had told a local farmer William Slater that Helgelien wouldn't bother Ray anymore because they had fixed him for keeps. Helgelien had of course disappeared like many others, and his brother, Asle Helgelien was making enquiries of Belle of his whereabouts. Belle replied to his letter stating that his brother was not residing at her farm and that perhaps he had returned to Norway to see relatives. Asle didn't believe this story, and felt his brother was still in La Porte. Belle responded again and said that if he wanted to come and search for his brother she would assist, but at a price.

Now that Ray had made comments about Helgelien to William Slater, and with the enquiries being made by Asle Helgelien, the heat was starting to turn up for Belle. If the truth of Helgelien's whereabouts came out, it would surely send Belle to the gallows. If someone started snooping around the farm, and asking questions about the men that had last been heard of there, Belle's life would be over. She had to take action.

Setting the Scene

The knowledge Ray had presented a very real danger to Belle, and so began the stage setting for the fire. Belle visited a lawyer called M.E. Leliter in La Porte and stated that she feared for the lives of herself and her children. She claimed that Ray had threatened to murder her and burn down the farm house. Because of this threat, she wanted to make out a last will and testament, just in case Ray went through with his threat.

Leliter drew up Belle's will, leaving her entire estate to the children. Belle then went to the bank which held the farm's mortgage, and paid off the debt. What Belle did not do, was go to the police and report the threats allegedly made by Ray. If someone was seriously threatening your life, to the point where you go and ensure you have a will drawn up, surely you would report the threat to the local authorities? For this reason, it is believed that there was never any threat made, and that Belle was just putting in place enough suspicion that she could get away with her final act of murder.

CHAPTER 6:
Burning Down the House

The farm house burnt to the ground in the early hours of the 28th of April, 1908. Within the ruins four bodies were found, three of which were Belle's children, and the fourth being an adult female, supposedly Belle. But there was an issue with the adult female's body, and one that would haunt the people of La Porte for decades to come.

The Headless Corpse

The body of the adult female found in the fire debris was missing a vital part of the anatomy, necessary for proof of identification – the head. People naturally assumed the body would be that of Belle, but they were not aware of the murderous crimes she had been committing at that stage. Instead the majority of the population of La Porte felt that it was just a tragic incident that took the lives of an innocent woman and her three children.

It wasn't until the doctors started to examine the body that things started to look more suspect. The first issue was the missing head, which would indicate that the woman had been murdered and decapitated before the fire was started. But none of the bodies of the children showed any signs of violent murder, so the question was asked why Belle should have been killed in such a way.

When the doctors measured the size and weight of the adult female, things got even more puzzling. They had measured the body as being five foot three inches in height, with a weight of 150 pounds at the most. Those who knew Belle knew that this couldn't be possible, as she had been a large woman, almost six feet tall, and weighed closer to 200 pounds.

Neighbors, friends, and the local garment manufacturers all stated that there was no way this body belonged to Belle. With the discrepancy in size, and weight, the authorities determined that the headless corpse was indeed not the remains of Belle. Also, the stomach contents of the victim were analyzed, and a pathologist found that the internal organs contained high doses of the poison strychnine.

Three weeks after the farm house had burnt down, some teeth were found amongst the debris. The teeth consisted of an upper and lower bridge, and Belle's dentist identified them as work he had done for her. As well as the dentures, there were also natural teeth found containing gold, and these too were identified as belonging to Belle. The metals contained in the dental work showed no damage from the fire, leading some to wonder if perhaps they had been planted there afterwards by someone wanting to put an end to the suspicion.

Witness Account

When Joe Maxson the farmhand awoke on the morning of the fire, he first thought that the smell of smoke was coming from the kitchen and that Belle must have been cooking breakfast. But as he lay in bed, and the smell got stronger, he realized it was something more serious. He got up, put on his slippers, and poked his head out of the window. He noticed puffs of smoke arising from the kitchen area, and each cloud seemed to get darker and darker. Suddenly realizing the house was on fire, he quickly put on his robe and tried to leave his bedroom, only to find that the handle was already hot and the door would not budge.

Although he seemed trapped, his first thoughts were of the sleeping children and Belle. He shouted out to them to try and wake them, listening all the while at the keyhole to see if he could hear them crying out or moving. A minute or two later, as his own room filled with smoke, he knew he had to get out, so he managed to find his way to the servant's stairs and made his escape.

Joe continued to circle around the outside of the house, yelling at the top of his voice to try and rouse Belle and the children. He looked for a window that he could climb through to try and rescue them, but each one was already blocked by flames. By now he had already accepted that Belle and the children were most likely to have perished. At this time, Belle was 48 years old, her daughter Myrtle was 11, Lucy was 9 and little Philip was just 5 years old.

Too Late

Two neighbors of Belle, Mike Clifford and William Humphrey, had noticed the fire from their property and made their way on bicycles to offer assistance. Along with Joe, they repeatedly tried to wake up the woman and her children inside the house by yelling, and throwing bricks that were lying nearby at the house. Clifford and Joe tried to break down the front door which was locked, but they had no success.

Humphrey located a ladder by the barn, and propped it up against the wall. Climbing up, he looked in every window he could, but could not see any signs of life. More neighbors arrived, the Laphams, Hutsons and Nicholsons. They joined the other men in yelling to try and alert Belle and her children, until they reached the conclusion that if they hadn't been heard, then those inside the house were most likely deceased.

The local Sheriff arrived from La Porte, along with a whole brigade of firemen, but by then it was far too late. The house, the outbuildings and even the nearby elm trees were all destroyed by the fire.

CHAPTER 7:
Digging Up the Truth

Although there had been plenty of suspicion regarding the identity of the woman's body found in the fire, this had largely been pushed aside until the Sheriff was visited by Asle Helgelien. This visit would result in a deeply disturbing revelation and discovery.

A Man with a Suspicion

Asle Helgelien was the brother of Andrew Helgelien, who had disappeared after visiting Belle. Asle had corresponded with Belle about the whereabouts of his brother, but Belle had denied any knowledge of his location, other than perhaps he had returned to Norway. Asle never believed this story, and when he read in the paper about the fire and the assumed death of Belle, he felt compelled to travel to La Porte to try and solve the mystery of his brother's disappearance.

There had been dozens of letters sent back and forth between Andrew, after he had answered her advertisement for a husband. She had portrayed herself as a decent woman, but as the letters increased, the tone of her writing suggested she was more interested in financial gain than anything else. When Andrew decided he was going to visit Belle, she instructed him not to send her any money through the bank, as she claimed banks were untrustworthy. She suggested he sew his paper money to the inside of his underwear, and that he should not tell a single soul of what he was doing.

Asle could not understand how his brother could have kept up correspondence for so long with Belle, and then withdraw all his savings and travel to visit her just to disappear without a trace. He was convinced something untoward had occurred. The Sheriff felt that Asle was wrong, because Belle was not a murderer or a gold digger in his opinion. It was then up to Asle to try and solve the mystery, and because he was aware of digging going on at the property and numerous personal items being found, he decided to offer his services to help.

A Gruesome Discovery

Operating on a hunch, Asle approached Joe Maxson and Daniel Hutson and offered to help them with the digging at the farm. Straight away, he asked Joe if he knew of any holes Belle had dug on the property since January, the month of which Andrew went missing. Maxson pointed out an area behind the farmhouse and near the pig pen where Belle had created a garbage pit, and he himself had covered it over around March at Belle's request.

Asle grabbed a shovel and without saying a word he started digging in that area. Curious, the other two men followed him over, and they all dug in what was once the garbage pit. As they began to dig deeper, they noticed an unpleasant smell emanating amongst the old boots and garbage. The smell became stronger, and before long they found a lump covered in an old sack and oilcloth. They removed the covering, and discovered a human arm. More body parts were removed from their hiding place, and finally they came across a man's head. Asle took one look at the features and announced they had found his brother.

The body of Andrew Helgelien had been completely dismembered, and each part had been shoved into various produce and flour sacks. The Sherriff was notified immediately, and attended the scene, as the men continued to dig. By the end of the day, they had found four more victims, two of which were male and the other two female. All had been dismembered and disposed of in the same manner as Andrew, and they were all shocked to discover that one of the females was actually Belle's foster daughter Jennie.

The Town Reacts

As news of the discovery of five bodies drifted through the county of La Porte, the people reacted in utter shock, terror and dismay. Many of the locals had thought of Belle as being a lonely woman, who had sadly buried two husbands and was running a farm and raising her children on her own. Little did they know that the body count was going to rise quite substantially.

At first the sheriff tried to keep the news quiet, but before long it had become national news. Poor, quiet La Porte was flooded with media personnel, with extra trains being organized to transport reporters in. They came from both near and far and more or less commandeered the largest hotel in town as their gathering place and news center.

Reporters went back and forth to the farm, trying to glean more information for their newspapers. They questioned every local person they came across to find out more about this terrible woman called Belle. A lot of the local residents stated how shocked they were, that they couldn't believe she could have done such horrible deeds. However, many claimed that now that they had thought about Belle, they did think she acted suspiciously on occasion. This could have been more to do with the psychological effect of the discovery rather than actual fact.

Now that the secrets surrounding Belle's disappearing suitors had been revealed, the people of La Porte and indeed other counties and cities, eagerly waited for news. They hoped and prayed the head of Belle would be found buried amongst the others, so they would then know she was definitely dead. If it was true that Belle had escaped the fire, they hoped she would be apprehended and punished, and some came to refer to Belle as the Black Widow of Indiana.

Skeletons Abound

They continued to dig up the land at Belle's farm through the month of May. More bodies were found, and the list of missing persons got longer and longer. Many of the victims had been decapitated, and most had been dismembered, probably for ease of burial. There were bodies of men and children, and a number of woman's accessories, later believed to belong to the headless corpse found in the house fire.

A lot of the human remains were never able to be identified, and because of this, bodies were buried together in coffins rather than having individual plots. Back in those days, body recovery wasn't the science it is today, so the methods of gathering the body parts were rather crude. At this time, they estimated they had found twelve victims buried on the farm.

CHAPTER 8:
Suspicion and Speculation

Once people became aware that Belle seemed to have gotten away with murder for such a long time, suspicions were aroused regarding the deaths of her former husbands. There was much speculation, both by the authorities and the people who knew Belle, and the relatives of the victims.

The Deaths of Her Husbands

The death of Belle's first husband, Mads Sorenson, had raised suspicion previously, especially for one of the doctors who investigated his death. Eight years earlier, Mads had died suddenly, and Dr. J.B. Miller was convinced he showed signs of strychnine poisoning. He had mentioned it to a superior at the time, but it was never taken any further. Dr. Miller's superior felt that because Mads had been treated for a heart problem, the most likely cause of death was enlargement of the heart, and he signed the death certificate.

Dr. Miller stated that this doctor had felt sorry for Belle, and had referred to her as a 'basket case' over her husband's death, so essentially an autopsy was avoided because of Belle's upset. But Dr. Miller was never convinced, and when he considered the evidence of poisoning along with the timing of the insurance policies, he was certain Belle had murdered her husband for the money.

When her second husband Peter Gunness died suddenly, again suspicions were raised concerning the cause of death. Belle's explanation of the falling meat grinder made no sense, as there was no logical reason for that piece of machinery to fall from the shelf. A legal hearing was held into the matter, with Belle putting on quite the performance of wailing in sorrow for her dead husband.

Even Belle's children were questioned about the death of Peter, and at one point, there was speculation regarding the true cause of death of Peter's infant child he brought with him to the relationship. Despite all of the allegations and the suspicion around Peter's death, the verdict was given as an accidental death.

It wouldn't be until after young Myrtle perished in the fire that a statement she made to a school friend would be brought to the attention of the authorities. The friend was sworn to secrecy, but once Myrtle had died, she no longer felt the need to keep the secret. This statement by Myrtle would have had a major impact on the verdict, and could have prevented Belle from continuing her killing spree. Just a week before the farm house burnt down, Myrtle had told her friend that her mother had killed her father with a meat cleaver.

The Alleged Victims

Although many of these victims were confirmed, some are alleged victims because of circumstances, such as their bodies not being found or identified.

Ole B. Budsberg - had left Wisconsin to visit Belle as a suitor.

Thomas Lindboe – moved from Chicago three years earlier to work on the Gunness farm.

Henry Gurholdt – also from Wisconsin, Henry had visited Belle with the promise of marriage, taking a sum of $1,500 with him. A watch that was the same as his was found with one of the bodies.

Olaf Svenherud – from Chicago, possibly one of Belle's suitors from the advertisements.

John Moe – from Minnesota, his watch was located in Ray Lamphere's possession.

Olaf Lindbloom – also from Wisconsin.

William Mingay – left New York City in April 1904 and disappeared, assumed a victim of Belle's.

Herman Konitzer – disappeared in January 1906.

Charles Edman – disappeared, was from New Carlisle, Indiana.

George Berry – this victim could have been a misspelt name of a known victim of Belle's called George Bradley, who had gone to La Porte to meet a widow who had three children.

Christie Hilkven – sold his farm in Wisconsin and moved to La Porte in 1906.

Chares Neiburg – a Scandinavian immigrant from Philadelphia had told friends he was going to visit Belle and disappeared.

John H. McJunkin – had been writing letters with a woman from La Porte, and left his wife in 1906 supposedly to meet her.

Olaf Jensen – another Norwegian immigrant, he notified his relatives by letter that he was leaving Indiana to marry a wealthy widow from La Porte.

Henry Bizge – disappeared from La Porte in June, 1906, along with his hired man Edward Canary.

Bert Chase – the owner of a butcher shop in Indiana, he sold his business and told friends he was going to meet a wealthy widow. His brother received a telegram telling him he had perished in a train accident, but this was later found to be fake.

Tonnes Peterson Lien – disappeared on the 2nd of April 1907. Was from Minnesota.

T.J. Tiefland – allegedly travelled from Minneapolis in 1907 to visit Belle.

Frank Riedinger – a Wisconsin farmer went to Indiana to marry in 1907 and disappeared.

Emil Tell – originally from Sweden, he left Missouri in 1907 to travel to La Porte.

Lee Porter – left his wife in Oklahoma and told his brother he was going to La Porte to marry a wealthy widow.

John E. Hunter – disappeared in November 1907from Pennsylvania, had told his daughters he was leaving to marry a wealthy widow in Indiana.

George Williams – also from Pennsylvania had told associates he was moving to the West to marry.

Ludwig Stoll – another from Pennsylvania who also said he was going to marry a woman in the West.

Abraham Phillips – a railway worker from West Virginia, Abraham went to Indiana to marry a wealthy widow in Indiana. A railway watch was found in the fire debris.

Benjamin Carling – left Chicago after telling his wife he was traveling to La Porte to visit a wealthy widow and secure an investment. His remains were subsequently identified by his wife.

Aug. Gunderson – from Wisconsin, disappeared.

Ole Oleson – from Michigan, disappeared.

Lindner Nikkelsen – from South Dakota, disappeared.

Andrew Anderson – from Kansas, disappeared.

Johann Sorenson – from Missouri, disappeared.

A man named 'Hinkley' was a possible victim.

The Unnamed Victims:

A gold ring was found after the fire with the marking: 'S.B. May 28, 1907'.

Mrs. H. Whitzer's daughter had gone to university close to La Porte in 1902.

A man and a woman who were unidentified disappeared the same night as Jennie. Belle had claimed a professor and his wife had come and taken Jennie to California.

Miss Jennie Graham's brother had left their home in Wisconsin to marry a wealthy widow in La Porte but disappeared.

An unknown man who was aged 50 and who worked as a hired hand disappeared, but Belle inherited his horse and buggy.

An unnamed gentleman from Montana had told people he was going to see Belle to sell her his horse and buggy. He disappeared, and the horse and buggy were found on Belle's farm.

CHAPTER 9:
Ray's Arrest

There were other victims of Belle's actions, besides those that met a grisly death at her hands. One of these victims was Ray Lamphere, her former farmhand, and the man she deliberately framed for the fire. Ray was arrested on the 22nd of May, 1908, and charged with the murder of Belle and her children, and arson for setting fire to the farmhouse.

The Trial

The trial of Ray Lamphere began on the 13th of November, after he had been held in custody since his arrest in May. Naturally, Ray stuck to his story of innocence, pleading not guilty to the crimes he was alleged to have committed. For the prosecution, the state's attorney Ralph N. Smith took charge of the case, and Ray was defended by Wirt Worden. The judge overseeing the trial was Judge J.C. Richter.

The case hinged on the prosecution's ability to convince the jury that the headless corpse found in the ruins of the fire was indeed that of Belle Gunness. In response, the defense would try to prove that it was not Belle that died in that fire, and they had a lot of evidence from witnesses and experts to back up that claim. Most of the prosecutor's evidence was circumstantial; mainly regarding the statements Belle had made to the lawyer and friends that she believed Ray was going to kill her and her children.

This trial was set to be a challenge from the start, with so many contributing factors and mystery surrounding the deeds of Belle, and whether or not it was she who was found in the remnants of the farmhouse following the fire. The body count had risen dramatically since the first victims were found buried, and the thoughts and feelings of the general public of the area were still very raw, as they tried to come to terms with what had been happening right under their noses.

Each day of the trial, the small courtroom was filled to the brim of both supporters of Ray, and those who had known Belle on a personal level. There were those who attended out of curiosity, and those who were disgusted by the alleged murders of Belle and her children by this man Ray Lamphere. Despite the emotions pervading those in the courtroom, the trial went ahead without disruption from the spectators.

The Prosecution

The whole basis of the prosecution's case was that Ray had deliberately murdered Belle out of revenge for firing him, and the lighting of the fire was to try and conceal the crime. There was also the suggestion of unrequited love, with Belle dismissing Ray's approaches whilst all the while romancing other men that came regularly to the farm.

The prosecution also put forward the suggestion that Ray not only helped Belle commit the murders, including that of Andrew Helgelien, but that he also was aware of the bodies buried on the farm. The first witnesses the prosecution intended on calling were those who had attended the scene of the fire immediately after it was discovered. One of these witnesses was William Humphrey, the neighbor who along with Joe Maxson had desperately tried to wake the assumed to be sleeping Belle and her children. This would prove to be detrimental to the prosecution's case, as there had been an account given by a female witness that claimed she saw the bodies huddled together on a bed. Following is an excerpt of the questioning directed at Humphrey:

Smith: At what time did you reach the scene of the fire?

Humphrey: At a few minutes after four in the morning.

Smith: What did you see, Mr. Humphrey?

Humphrey: William Clifford and Joe Maxson were just breaking in the front door. I climbed up a ladder and looked in the windows of the two rooms on the west side. I saw mattresses and bed clothing, but no people...Soon, the walls began to fall, and the roof caved in.

Smith: Were you present when the bodies were found?

Humphrey: Yes, sir, it was my shovel that struck one of them. I assisted in taking them out and placing them in the undertaker's wagon.

Smith: You say you looked in the window during the fire, Mr. Humphrey. What exactly did you see?

Humphrey: In the first room there was an iron bed with bare mattresses. In the second room there was an iron bed with mattress and some sort of a small bundle of bed clothing on it.

Smith: Was the room on fire?

Humphrey: The fire was beginning to come through the floor.

Straight away, the testimony of the female witness was brought into question. If Humphrey had seen the beds clear with no bodies on them, how could they have been found together on a mattress? Sheriff Smutzer had also claimed he had seen the bodies of the victims lying together on a mattress, though his description included words such as petrified, pitiful, and frozen in pain, probably to make a bigger impact on the jury.

The prosecutor also called to the witness stand men who socialized and drank with Ray to testify regarding the threats they had heard him make on occasion towards Belle. Nowadays of course, statements made while under the influence of alcohol would not be given as much credence as they may have been back in the early 1900s.

The Defense

The whole structure and success of the defense relied on convincing the jury that the headless corpse found in the burnt out house was not the body of Belle. Murder at that time was a hangable offense so the priority was to save the neck of Ray Lamphere.

It would have been difficult to fight the charges by trying to show that Ray had no ill feelings towards Belle. There had been too many occasions where Belle had told the locals about Ray threatening her or making a nuisance of himself. Also, Ray had been arrested numerous times due to Belle's allegations. So instead of portraying Ray as a good decent man who wouldn't harm Belle and her children, the defense set about debunking previous witness statements regarding the identification of the body.

The biggest item of evidence produced by the prosecution was the teeth that were found after the fire, supposedly belonging to Belle. Although they weren't discovered until three weeks after the fire, Belle's personal dentist insisted they were hers, as he recognized his own handiwork. The dentist had also claimed that the real teeth found would have been impossible for Belle to pull out by herself.

It was going to be difficult to convince the jury that Belle had in fact pulled her own teeth out and left them along with her dentures so that they may be found after the fire. Any rational person would find it appalling even considering pulling their own teeth. Dentures of course are easily replaceable, and a person can live without them, but their own teeth? Imagine the pain, strength and discomfort of performing that act on oneself.

Wirt Worden sought the opinions and testimony of a local jeweler, due to the amount of gold inlaid in Belle's bridgework. The jeweler testified that the gold was almost completely undamaged, and yet other items in the house that had contained gold or had been gold plated had melted due to the severe heat of the fire.

Gold is a soft metal, and it melts quite easily. To prove this point, a replication of the dental bridgework had been attached to a human jawbone and put into the forge of a blacksmith. The natural teeth disintegrated under the heat, the gold had melted, and the teeth that were porcelain were damaged also. This evidence showed that there was no possible way Belle's teeth, both her natural teeth and her dentures, could not have survived that fire unscathed. Then how did they get there? Another theory came up during the testimony of two witnesses.

During the questioning of Joe Maxson and another witness, both had claimed they had seen the sheriff place the bridgework at the scene of the fire. He allegedly had the teeth and dentures in his pocket, and placed them on the ground, and shortly thereafter, they were discovered. Why the sheriff would have done this or how he came to be in possession of the teeth remains a mystery, and it was never proven.

Was There A Body Double?

Another angle the defense tackled was the testimony of John Anderson who lived just down the road from Belle's farm. Anderson was very well respected throughout the community, and was considered an individual of high standing. His testimony would put question into whether or not it was possible for Belle to have killed an innocent woman and placed her body into the house before it was set alight, in order to fake her own death.

The most important part of the questioning of Anderson by Worden went as follows:

Worden: Mr. Anderson, did you see Mrs. Gunness shortly before the fire?

Anderson: Yes, I did, on the Saturday evening before the fire. She was driving by in her buggy, and she stopped to ask how the flowers were getting along.

Worden: Was anybody with her?

Anderson: There was a strange woman with her.

Worden: Describe her, please, Mr. Anderson.

Anderson: She was a large woman, not quite as large as Mrs. Gunness.

Worden: Did you ever see her again?

Anderson: Never. After the fire I told the sheriff about her.

The entire courtroom gasped in shock at this revelation, and more than likely instilled fear into many of those present, at the thought that this terrible murderer may still be alive. The description of the mystery woman matched the size and weight of the victim of the fire, and was certainly a better match than the larger size of Belle. It was also taken into consideration that the Sherriff had never mentioned the statement by Anderson to anyone, which shone a poor light on the prosecution.

Another witness, a fellow called Daniel Hutson, was also brought to the stand to give his statement. Hutson lived nearby and at one point had even worked for Belle on her farm. His evidence was as follows:

Worden: Have you seen Mrs. Gunness since the fire?

Hutson: On the road near the hog pen.

Worden: What date did you see her?

Hutson: On the ninth day of July. I was coming from town with a hayrack, and I saw through the trees Mrs. Gunness and a man walking in the orchard. Even at that distance, I could recognize her plainly. I knew her size, I knew her shape, and I knew her lumbering walk. I never saw another woman who walked like her. She had on a light skirt, black waist, a wide-trimmed hat with a black veil that came down to the chin and a white veil over that. There was a man with her. He weighed about 165 pounds. He had a gray mustache and gray hair.

Worden: What did you do?

Hutson: I started up my horses to try to get up the hill to the orchard before she could get away, but when I got within two wagon lengths of the buggy, they ran to it, clambered in, and raced straight for the main road. I tried to follow them, but they got ahead of me, and I did not like to follow them anymore. There was a good chance of me getting a chunk of lead!

Now there was a witness statement claiming to have seen Belle after the fire in the company of an unknown man. Of note, Hutson also described this man as not resembling Ray Lamphere. Did Belle have an accomplice? Many were beginning to think so. Maybe that's who pulled out her teeth? This sighting was also backed up by two boys who claimed to have seen a woman wearing two veils on the same day as Hutson. Both of Hutson's daughters also claimed they had seen Belle and a strange man during July on more than one occasion. On one of these occasions, Belle was described as wearing two veils, one of which was a black veil, and the woman was trying to hide her face.

The last witness for the defense was Dr. Walter Haines, who was a toxicology professor. Dr. Haines took the stand on the 24th of November to give evidence regarding the stomach contents of Andrew Helgelien. He had also been asked to analyze the stomach contents of the Gunness children and the headless woman. Unfortunately this analysis was flawed, as all of the stomachs had been stored in the same jar in solution, so even though large amount of strychnine were found, Dr. Haines could not prove which of the stomachs it came from.

One important piece of information that was given by Dr. Haines however was that embalming fluid did not contain strychnine. The prosecution team had previously stated that this was the case, so the defense was able to clarify this for the jury.

Verdict

At the end of the trial, the prosecution called for the death penalty to be bestowed upon Ray Lamphere for the murders, whereas the defense in their closing statement implored the jury to spare the life of Ray, due to the prosecution's evidence being purely circumstantial. The decision for the jury was a difficult one, and they were divided in their opinion. Eventually they came to a compromise, and by late afternoon on

Thanksgiving, all those involved were summonsed back to the court.

When asked for the verdict, the foreman of the jury admitted they had reached a decision, but they had a statement they would like to read before they gave the judge the verdict. The judge would not allow this statement to be made until after the verdict was given. The courtroom was completely silent, as people waited for the decision.

The foreman of the jury declared they had found Ray guilty of arson, but not murder. The statement they made was as follows:

"We hereby state that it was our judgment in the consideration of this case that the adult body found in the ruins of the fire was that of Belle Gunness and that the case was decided by us on an entirely different proposition."

Ray's neck had been saved after all. Although he would still go to prison, he at least would not go to the gallows. Interestingly, Worden would forever believe that the body in the fire was not Belle, and that she had made a cunning escape by faking her own death. Smith on the other hand, believed the complete opposite, that it had been Belle's body in the ruins of the fire.

Ray's sentence was given as being between two and twenty years in the state prison. The longest sentence was perhaps given to the people of La Porte, many of who believed that Belle was still alive, and so spent years living in fear.

CHAPTER 10:
Deathbed Stories

People who are facing death, whether it is by sickness or executioner, will often confess to any sins they may have committed. Some however, will take their secrets to the grave, which can be extremely frustrating and upsetting for the victims of crime who only want to know the truth. Deathbed confessions are usually truthful, and most of those who give them are looking for absolution before they pass away.

Ray Lamphere

Ray would barely spend a year behind bars in the state penitentiary. He developed tuberculosis, and near his death on the 30th of December of 1909, he called for a clergyman to come and see him. The Reverend E.A. Schell attended Ray and took his confession, then sealed it in a safe until after Ray died. Because of the tuberculosis, the governor of the state offered Ray a pardon, but only if he would tell the true story of what happened on that farm. Ray refused, and so he died within the prison walls.

The Reverend came forward with the confession on the 14th of January 1910, two weeks after Ray's death, and what was contained within the confession would be astonishing. Ray insisted that he had never murdered anyone, but he had assisted Belle after she had murdered the men.

According to Ray, when the men came to call, Belle would put on a charming act, making sure her visitor was comfortable and provided with a good meal. They would be given a cup of coffee, laced with poison, and once they entered into a drug-induced stupor, she would kill them by striking them in the head with a meat chopper. Other victims were sometimes killed by chloroform while they were sleeping, which is a much less violent manner, but murder nonetheless.

Once they were dead, Belle, being a large and strong woman, would take the bodies to the basement of the house and set about dismembering them. After the remains were placed in sacks and bags they would then be buried either in the grounds surrounding the farm house, or in the pig pen. Belle's former husband, Peter Gunness, was an accomplished butcher, so she had learnt her dismembering skills by watching him deal with the carcass of animals.

Occasionally Belle would dispose of the victims in a variety of other ways, including placing the corpse into the vat used for pig-scalding then covering them with quicklime. One of the worst methods described by Ray was that sometimes Belle would simply feed the pigs the remains. Pigs will devour almost anything, and they do so rather quickly, which would have made sure nothing would be seen or found.

Ray also admitted his role in the house fire, and the mystery surrounding the headless corpse. Apparently, Belle had pretended to hire a woman from Chicago as a housekeeper in the days leading up to the fire. Once this woman had arrived at the farm, Belle had drugged her and murdered her. According to Ray, she had taken the head and thrown it into a nearby swamp after weighing it down with weights.

Belle allegedly killed her children by using chloroform and smothering techniques before taking the bodies and placing them in the basement along with the body of the dead woman. To make the woman resemble her, Belle used her own clothing to dress the body and then placed her dentures nearby. She then set fire to the house and escaped.

Ray claimed that Belle was meant to meet him after lighting the fire, but she never showed up. Ray admitted that he had helped with the fire, but had nothing to do with the actual murders of the mystery woman and the children. He believed Belle had escaped across nearby fields and into the woods. There had been rumors at one point that Ray had admitted to some that he drove her to nearby Stillwell and put her on a train, but this was not confirmed by Ray.

Also in his confession was the reason behind the murders committed by Belle, according to Ray. She had apparently become a very wealthy woman, and the money had come from the estimated 42 men she had murdered. By Ray's estimate Belle had around $250,000, almost all of which was gained through deception and murder. Belle had more than enough money to ensure an escape and relocation.

Elizabeth Smith

A nearby resident was a woman called Elizabeth Smith, who was well known for practicing voodoo, and was Belle's closest friend in La Porte. During the trial of Ray, she had told his lawyer, Wirt Worden, that when she was near to death she would summon him and tell him everything she knew. She certainly tried to keep her promise, when she sent for Worden a few days before she died in 1916.

Unfortunately, Worden was on vacation in Louisiana when word reached him that Elizabeth was ready to see him. Despite his efforts to get back to La Porte, Elizabeth had passed away before he reached her, so her secrets were never known. After she died, workers were clearing out the debris in her house, which was quite rundown, and they came across an old skull. It was definitely human and covered in cobwebs, and because of the initial approach she mad to Worden, questions about this skull abounded.

Some wondered if the skull had belonged to the mystery woman who allegedly perished in the fire on Belle's farm. If so, did Ray give it to her to use in her voodoo rituals? Now that both Ray and Elizabeth were dead, nobody would ever know the truth about this skull.

CHAPTER 11:
Visions of Hell's Belle

The people of La Porte had given Belle a number of nicknames, including Lady Bluebeard, the Black Widow, and of course, Hell's Belle. Her violent and repeated acts of murder were to stay in the minds of the local people for many years, and some swore they saw her after her alleged death, while others feared they would see her.

Decades of Sightings

There were reports of numerous sightings of Belle for decades after the murders and the fire. Some of these were probably nonsense, such as the rumors of Belle being a brothel madam in the South. However, these sightings went on for nearly 25 years, and they were spread out all around the country.

There had been many witnesses who claimed to have seen Belle near her farm during the July following the fire. Some of these, as mentioned earlier, were highly esteemed members of the public, whose word would be taken in good stead. It is difficult to ascertain whether all of these sightings were legitimate, or whether they were a form of understandable paranoia considering the events that had taken place at that farm.

A delivery boy from La Porte claimed to have seen Belle at Elizabeth Smith's home three days after the house had burnt down and Belle had supposedly perished in the fire. He was apparently terrified of maybe being murdered by Belle himself, or because Elizabeth was well known for practicing voodoo, so he kept this information to himself for many years.

Belle was often reportedly seen in Chicago, New York, San Francisco and Los Angeles. Some of these sightings were told by people who actually knew Belle, which would have given credence to their stories. Investigators from La Porte were often summoned to various places around the country to explore the possibilities of these sightings being true. The police department apparently received two reports of sightings each month on average. There was also a reported sighting of Belle in 1931, in Mississippi, where she lived happily on a large piece of land. The final reported sighting of Belle also took place in 1931, when another woman called Esther Carlson was arrested in Los Angeles.

True Sightings or Were They Visions Driven by Fear?

While it is very possible that many of the early sightings were legitimate, it is hard to determine whether all of the reports were accurate. If one was to believe that Belle did not perish in the fire, then it is highly likely that many if not all of the sightings were actually Belle. It would be difficult to completely vanish off the face of the earth, especially when your crimes have become nationwide news.

Certainly Belle had the financial means and the cunning to get away from La Porte to somewhere far away. With so much money in her possession, she could have ended up anywhere. There were even suggestions that perhaps she returned to Norway, though this is less likely, given her terrible time there as a child.

Such a large number of people who personally knew Belle reported seeing her after the fire that it is hard to discount these accounts as being mistakes. She was certainly an imposing looking woman, bigger than many men, so it would be hard to mistake her for someone else. And then of course the confession made by Ray needs to be considered also. Why would he confess to assisting her not only with disposing of the bodies but of escaping as he died? He stood to gain nothing positive from the confession. If anything it would alter his own legacy and how people felt about him.

An impact on the psyche of the local people needs to be considered when trying to determine whether or not sightings were legitimate. The people of La Porte in particular were subjected to shock, horror and fear, and when the suggestion of Belle not dying in the fire came about, those feelings would have been intensified. Fear became a big part of many people's lives, always wondering if Belle would come back and murder again. For a very long time, the majority of the population of La Porte would not go out at night for this very reason.

So were some of the sightings the figment of a fearful imagination? It is hard to say for sure, but it would certainly be a very real possibility.

CHAPTER 12:
The Mystery of Esther Carlson

Just when things were starting to die down in the public's eye regarding Belle, another mystery surfaced that puzzled everyone for many years to come. It all started with the arrest of a woman in California, for the murder of a gentleman she had been working for as his housekeeper. The identity of this woman, and the mystery surrounding her existence, would once again have people believing that Belle had faked her own death in the fire.

A Question of Murder

A gentleman by the name of August Lindstrom died supposedly from a heart attack on the 9th of February 1931. He resided in Lomita, California, and had a live-in housekeeper called Esther Carlson. Esther had started working for August Lindstrom following the death of her husband in 1925. By the time of Lindstrom's death, Esther had managed to convince him to add her name to his bank account.

It wasn't until after his death that one of his sons had noticed some problems with the records of his father's account. When this information was combined with the fact that Esther's name was on the account, suspicions were ignited that Lindstrom hadn't died of natural causes, but rather that he was murdered. The most likely motive was money.

Acting on those suspicions, the son notified the appropriate authorities, and an exhumation of Lindstrom's body was ordered. Though buried in Arizona, the body was transported to the coroner's office in Los Angeles for an autopsy to be completed. Because it had been initially assumed to be a natural death, no previous autopsy had been conducted.

The autopsy of Lindstrom revealed that he had indeed been murdered, by arsenic poisoning. Straight away, the authorities brought Esther in for questioning. Another potential victim who was currently in the hospital with arsenic poisoning, was a close friend of Lindstrom's and Esther's, a woman called Anna Erickson. Despite being ill herself, Anna was also considered a suspect.

Both Esther and Anna had supposedly put pressure on the deputy coroner at the time of Lindstrom's death to issue the death certificate straight away. Because the cause of death was assumed to be a heart attack, the deputy coroner obliged with the request of the two women.

When the financial circumstances were investigated, not only was Esther's name on Lindstrom's account, but it was also on the title of the house they lived in. The day after his death,

Esther had arranged to withdraw the entire amount in the bank account, the sum of $2,000. At this time in history, such an amount was considered a fortune.

Once Anna started to recover from the arsenic poisoning, she claimed that she had gotten sick after having a cup of coffee at the Lindstrom residence after his death. She also claimed that Esther had caused Lindstrom's death, and had once stated that she was tired of taking care of old men. This led to Esther making her own allegations against Anna, and both of the women were held for further questioning. Subsequently, on the 24th of February, 1931, both Esther and Anna were charged with the murder of Lindstrom.

Esther was afflicted by tuberculosis, and her health deteriorated dramatically during April of that year. She was still awaiting her trial, and due to the gravity of her illness, the authorities questioned her relentlessly, even while she was on her deathbed. Still she insisted she was innocent of any wrongdoing.

The trial against Anna went ahead, beginning on the 30th of April. She would later be found not guilty of the murder, and nobody else was ever brought to trial for the crime. At this same time, suspicions had arisen among the authorities about the true identity of Esther, and it was announced that the prosecution team were calling witnesses forward from La

Porte. The authorities had begun to think that Esther Carlson was in fact Belle Gunness.

'I'm Convinced She's Belle'

When news of a woman aged in her 70s had been arrested and charged with murder, the Deputy Sheriff in La Porte, C.A. Fitzgerald organized for two of the former residents of La Porte who now lived in California to help the authorities determine whether or not Esther Carlson was indeed Belle Gunness.

The two gentlemen asked to assist were John A. Torkey and John 'Dennis' Daly. They had both known Belle well during the time they lived in La Porte and could easily recognize her by sight. A photograph of Esther was shown to Torkey, because she was too unwell to receive any type of visitors. He stated it certainly looked like Belle, but the photograph didn't show the wart Belle had on her face.

Photographs taken commercially back then were often touched up, with defects or flaws erased, so the negative of the original photo was obtained by the police. This clearly showed that there was a wart on the woman's face.

Both Torkey and Daly were taken to view Esther's body in the morgue after she had passed away. Daly was adamant that the woman was Belle, and he would know because he had talked to her in his words, 'hundreds of times' during his stay in La Porte. Torkey also agreed that Esther was in fact Belle.

The features that Torkey claimed proved to him it was Belle were her mouth, the eyes, eyebrows and hair. Belle had a slight twist to her mouth, just like the body in the morgue. The eyes were said to look the same as Belle's did. The color of the hair and the eyebrows had aged and faded, but they still looked like Belle's.

When the authorities looked into Esther Carlson's background, they discovered they could find no records of her whatsoever prior to 1908. This further indicated that she was not who she claimed to be, as there should have been some information on her. Despite the positive identifications by both Torkey and Daly, Esther's friends denied the possibility that she was Belle Gunness. They claimed Esther had originally emigrated from Sweden, and her name had been Esther Johnson. They also stated that during the period of Belle's acts of murder, Esther had been working in Connecticut as a housekeeper.

With so many contradictions, the mystery of Esther's true identity would remain unsolved. It wasn't until 2007 that investigators would try once more to solve the puzzle. Those that believed she was Belle Gunness were relieved following her death, as now they knew that they were finally rid of the terrifying Lady Bluebeard.

DNA Testing

In 2007, a group of graduate students and forensic anthropologists from the University of Indianapolis set about trying to solve the mystery of Belle Gunness and Esther Carlson using DNA analysis. A sister of Belle gave permission for the team to exhume the grave containing the body believed to be the remains of Belle found after the farm house fire. A surprise awaited them all on opening the coffin.

There were bones of children mixed in with the woman's bones in the coffin, yet there were no records of any children having been buried with her. This discovery suggested that the bones had been mixed up when collected from the burned ruins of the house, further suggesting the whole investigation had been poor and lacking. The bones comprised of the skeletons of two children, aside from the three of Belle's children who were buried in separate graves

If the bones had been mixed up, then there was the distinct possibility that there could have been other children buried beneath the floor of the farmhouse. If it is true that Belle had murdered more children, one would have to wonder where they came from, and why their disappearances hadn't been reported. There were no other known biological children belonging to Belle, and it was not known if Belle had fostered any other children.

As well as exhuming the body for the purposes of extracting DNA, an envelope was received from one victim's family. The envelope had originally contained a letter sent by Belle to a suitor, and it was hoped that when she licked the envelope flap she left some of her DNA behind. Unfortunately, the envelope was too old, and no useable DNA was found.

To date, all DNA testing has proven to be inconclusive as to the identity of the headless corpse, and whether or not it was Belle Gunness in that coffin. There has also been no confirmation through DNA testing as to whether or not Esther Carlson was really Belle. Despite this, the investigation is still ongoing, and the team hopes to one day find the answer through modern technology.

CHAPTER 13:
A Researcher's Discovery

A researcher from Norway called Knut Erik Jensen had dedicated much of his time to investigating whether Belle and Esther were the same woman. Knut had a strange connection to both women, as he had come from the same town as Belle, and at one point had lived nearby to the Esther's final resting place in Palm Springs.

Knut set about trying to either confirm links between the two women, or debunk the theories that had circulated for more than 100 years. It is undeniable that there were uncanny similarities between Belle and Esther, from the way they looked to the way they killed. When the suggestion first arose in 1931 that they were the same woman, much of this supposition was based on the unknown history of Esther.

Through his investigative research, Knut had discovered quite a bit about Esther's past leading up to the murder of Lindstrom. Disturbingly, her past echoed Belle's in many ways. Esther had used a number of names and aliases throughout her life, including Augusta Carlson, Esther Hanson, Augusta Hanson,

Esther Johnson and Augusta Johnson. It is believed that when she first came to America she was using the name Esther Augusta Johnson. Records of an Augusta Johnson were found that showed her having moved from Sweden to America in 1892, and at that time she was employed by a family in Hartford.

The Husbands

Esther's first husband was a man called Charles Hanson. Hanson died by drowning just nine months into their marriage. Their marriage took place in 1907, at the same time that Belle was residing in La Porte. There is no information about the circumstances of her husband's drowning so it is difficult to conclude that it may have been murder.

In 1911 Esther married her second husband, a man by the name of Charles Carlson. They were married in Arizona, and the marriage would last until the death of Charles in 1925. Charles had suffered an illness for an extraordinary 18 long months before his death, and his cause of death was listed as stomach cancer. This mirrors the circumstances of the man who first assaulted Belle and caused her miscarriage. Same symptoms, same diagnosis.

There was a gentleman living with Belle and Charles Carlson by the name of Gustav Ahlzen. When he died, it was ruled a suicide, as it was believed Gustav had consumed a bottle of strychnine poison. This would have been difficult to rule as a murder, as the poison of choice for most female murderers was strychnine.

Finally there was the death of August Lindstrom, due to poisoning by arsenic. Also there was the attempted poisoning of her close friend and alleged partner, Erikson. It was believed that Esther used to serve arsenic in split pea soup, which most likely would have hidden the taste. Belle preferred to serve strychnine in coffee.

Age Discrepancies

An Arizona census from 1910 showed that Esther was aged 30 years at that time. The California census from 1920 listed her as being 40 years of age. Considering the age of Belle at the time of the fire in 1908 was 48 years of age, there is quite a big difference between the two women. However, records on Belle weren't entirely true and factual, and many people who knew Belle had no clue how old she really was, so it is possible that she was younger than was thought.

Family Identifications

The man who organized all of the arrangements for Esther's funeral was called Michael Byrnes. It was claimed that he was married to Esther's sister, and further research showed that there was indeed a man by that name married to a woman whose maiden name was Johnson, and they lived in Hartford. Michael Byrnes declared on viewing the body in the morgue that it most certainly was the body of Esther, What isn't known, is how long he had known Esther for – was it possible he was mistaken?

Two other family members had a different opinion on the identity of the woman known as Esther. One was descended from Lindstrom, Pat Shawler, and the other was a descendent of Belle's sister Nellie, called Suzanne McKey. Both claimed that the two women, Belle and Esther, were one and the same.

The Photograph

In a trunk amongst Esther's belongings, a photograph was found of three children. Esther claimed to have never had any children, so where did the photograph come from? Who were the children? It was known that Belle had three children; therefore a lot of people put two and two together and decided it was a photo of Belle's children, and so Esther was actually Belle. But, the Byrnes side of the family had a lot of daughters, and suggestion has been made that the photograph was of three of the Byrne's girls. This was never confirmed however.

Knut's Conclusion

Although there were so many coincidences between the lives of Belle and Esther, the research conducted by Knut led him to decide that they were not the same person. The age differences, location discrepancies, family identifications, and the fact that he could find records on Esther that others claimed didn't exist, all convinced him of there having been two murderous women, not just one.

CHAPTER 14:
A New Theory to Consider

There is one possible theory that hasn't really been considered, until now. If so many people could not tell the difference between Esther and Belle, then perhaps one of them used that to their own advantage. Maybe one assumed the identity of the other as part of the escape.

The Body Without a Head

The headless corpse found in the aftermath of the fire holds the key to the story. Let's look at the facts:

- The body was smaller and lighter than Belle
- The teeth were undamaged despite being in a roaring house fire
- The head was missing

Those who knew Belle well swore that the body that was burned in the fire could not possibly have been her. Belle was a large, imposing woman, standing nearer to six feet and weighing allegedly more than 200 pounds. The headless body was not only shorter, but weighed a lot less, even when the effects of the fire were taken into consideration.

As shown during the trial of Ray Lamphere, the bridgework that supposedly belonged to Belle still had gold set in it even after the fire. Re-creations proved that at that temperature created by the fire, gold would melt. With the dentures, it was also proven that porcelain teeth were easily damaged by fire, leaving them with pock marks and pits. Also, the natural teeth that belonged to Belle should have crumbled from the heat, yet they were still intact. This would all indicate that the teeth and dentures were placed after the fire. There was a reported sighting of the sheriff pulling the teeth out of his pocket and placing them near the remains three weeks after the fire, but this was neither confirmed nor denied.

The first theory following the fire was that Ray Lamphere, who was angry with Belle, murdered her children with chloroform, then cut off Belle's head and set fire to the house. First of all, if Ray was angry with Belle, why would he kill her children? They had done him no harm. Although perhaps he saw them as witnesses. There was also no way he could have killed the children first – Belle would have killed him before he had a chance to kill her. Ray of course was found innocent by trial of the murders, but there were suggestions, even by him on his deathbed, that he had been an accomplice of some sort.

So, if someone had murdered Belle and chopped off her head, what did they do with it? If they simply wanted to cut her head off out of revenge or hatred, why wouldn't they have just left it to burn in the fire with the rest of the human remains? The only logical answer was that the head was removed to prevent identification, and the only person that would gain from that, was Belle.

The Mystery Man and Woman

There were two mystery people in La Porte immediately before the day of the fire, and within the first few months following. It wasn't a big town, so when strangers entered, people took notice. Witnesses claimed to have seen Belle with an unknown woman the day before the fire. Nobody had a clue who this woman was, or why she was with Belle. She was never seen again after the fire, so it can be assumed that maybe she was the headless corpse.

After the fire, there were a few sightings of Belle around July, in the company of a gentleman who was unknown. They were seen riding in a buggy each time and the woman always wore two veils, one of which was black, as though she was trying to conceal her face. A couple of witnesses caught a glimpse of her face when the veil lifted, and they were convinced that the woman was Belle.

The Dates

We know that the fire took place in 1908, and during the years leading up to the fire, Belle had been luring men to her farm with promises of marriage in exchange for money. She had advertised in many different newspapers, and there was a lot of response to her adverts. We also know that most of the men that responded and visited Belle were never seen again. What we don't know, is whether it was only men that replied, or whether couples also replied in the hopes of gaining work or money.

Switched Identity

So, when these things are all taken into consideration, it paints a very interesting picture. Esther's husband Charles, who she married in 1907, drowned only nine months into the marriage. Esther would have been alone and perhaps she had answered an advertisement in the newspaper that would take her to La Porte. Who knows, maybe Belle had advertised for a housekeeper. After all, that is what Esther done for work previously.

What if Belle had corresponded with Esther and they had exchanged photographs. This could have shown Belle whether or not they looked similar – similar enough to pass off as each other. Once Belle had lured Esther to her home, she could then be murdered, and put in place of Belle in the house as she burnt it down. Then, Belle could have simply escaped to Arizona and assumed Esther's identity.

There is no information regarding the drowning of Charles Hanson., including whether or not his body was found. If his body was missing, there could be another theory linking him to Belle. Suppose Charles felt he had made a mistake in marrying Esther, and on seeing an advertisement in the newspaper by a wealthy widow, he faked his death. Or, he could have just up and left, and the drowning was assumed.

Maybe once Charles met Belle he mentioned how similar she looked to Esther and the idea of swapping their identities came to Belle. Charles could have been the one who lured Esther to the farm. Many people will do almost anything for the right price, and Belle certainly had plenty of money. Once the murderous deed was done and the house was burned to the ground, Charles may have helped Belle escape and they could have laid low at Elizabeth Smith's house immediately following the fire. After all, the delivery boy claimed he saw her there and there were sightings of a man at the house as well.

Once they were assured it was safe to flee, they could have made their way back to Arizona where Belle may have taken on the identity of Esther. This would explain why there are records on Esther, as for all intents and purposes, she had at one time been a separate person, not just the same person as

Belle. Then, once Belle grew tired of Charles, she murdered him.

This is all purely conjecture of course, as there is no proof and it is only a theory, but it does make some sense. It would explain how Esther began to murder the men in her life with poison, just as Belle had done. And it would also explain why the women appeared so similar.

CHAPTER 15:
What Went Wrong With Belle?

A female serial killer is a lot less common than their male counterparts, and very few have reached double figures when it comes to victims. Some place Belle's true victim tally at around 48, which would make her the worst female serial killer in America, and around the world. Experts and civilians alike strive to try and understand what makes a serial killer do what they do, and researchers are always trying to find ways to prevent it from occurring.

A Clear Motive

The motive behind serial killers can vary between them, and the males typically murder out of some sexual perversion, hatred or frustration. Women on the other hand, often have completely different motives, possibly because they are the more emotional of the genders. This isn't a hard and fast rule however; there will always be exceptions to the rule.

Belle Gunness had a very clear motive almost right from the start. Her first possible victim was the man who assaulted her and caused her to have a miscarriage. Although the death was ascribed to cancer, his symptoms resembled those of poisoning. The motive for this victim would most likely have been revenge, whereas the others, who were to follow, were killed for money.

The marriage between Belle and her first husband lasted quite a while, and this is probably because throughout it they had been committing insurance fraud, so there was money coming in regularly. They even insured their first two children, shortly before they died in infancy, and received financial gain for their deaths. At some point greed consumed Belle, and instead of burning down their houses or business, she came up with the idea of insuring her husband and then murdering him by poison. She probably knew that he would have to be the victim, because if she murdered any more children, the insurance company and the authorities would become suspicious.

From that point on, Belle used men simply for their finances. She lured them by advertisements, and promises of marriage, in exchange for money. Every man she invited to meet her at the farm was instructed to bring money with him. Those that had no money were turned down. The ones that brought their savings with them, disappeared, ending up in the dirt beneath the pig pen.

Belle's incessant need for more money could stem from her childhood. Growing up in poverty, especially when a child is ridiculed for it, would drive many people to want to have more. Whilst some strive to attain it legitimately through work, it was extremely difficult for women to do this back then, as most were expected to stay at home and take care of the family. For Belle, the only way for her to become rich was to take it from other people.

Psychiatric State

It is no surprise that some would wonder if Belle had a psychiatric condition that caused her to kill so many people. There is no information on her mental health at all, and it was never mentioned by her friends and associates that she may have been mentally unwell. Still, even though spurred on by greed, it is hard to believe that a woman could do such horrific deeds and be of sound mind.

What made this story so horrifying was how she handled the bodies of the victims. She treated them like animal carcasses, carrying them to the basement and hacking them apart for easier disposal. Dismembering a body is a gruesome task, and there would have been blood and tissue all over that basement. Every time she swung the meat cleaver, body fluids would have been splattered everywhere. There are people who couldn't even do that to an animal, yet this woman did it to allegedly 40-odd human beings!

The ability of Belle to completely depersonalize the people she killed is astonishing. They were nothing to her, only money. To have the ability to feed body parts to her pigs late at night and feel nothing about it is bordering on inhuman. But was she insane? Not likely. She was calculating, she knew how to manipulate people, and she handled finance extremely well. She possibly planned her own fake death, her escape, and was able to continue living her life supposedly without getting caught. That shows a level of intelligence that few people would possess.

Emigration Effect

Hundreds of thousands of people emigrate, usually to escape poverty, politics, or in search of a better life for themselves. In the era of Belle Gunness, it was common for Europeans to move to America, and often they settled in communities where there were large numbers of others from the same country. Most people assume that moving to another country would be a positive experience, a new start, but often, it can have a more negative effect.

Research over the years has shown that the process of moving to another country can greatly affect the mental and physical health of an individual. Stress after all is a major contributor to many health problems. But it is more than just the stress of financing the trip, packing and moving.

Those who move to a country where their native language is not the primary language can find the language barrier hugely frustrating, frightening and embarrassing. It can be overwhelming to suddenly be in a place where there are a lot more people, especially for those like Belle who have come from a small, isolated town.

This type of mental impact can drown some people, and many can experience depression, and even grief, for those they left behind in their mother country. Family separation can cause a number of emotional issues, and once a person had emigrated, they very seldom made their way back to the place they came from. Belle was fortunate that her sister was already living in America, so she wasn't completely alone. It still would have been daunting however, and perhaps Belle manage this stress and anxiety by focusing on the one thing she loved the most – money.

CHAPTER 16:
A Woman without a Conscience

The dastardly deeds committed by Belle would have been repulsive and incomprehensible to normal citizens. Killing an adult perhaps may not be so much of a stretch, but killing young children, particularly those of your own, was just abominable. Belle used a variety of killing methods, some more violent than others, but the worst of it all was the dismemberment of the bodies and the way she disposed of them like they were trash.

The Use of Violence

Belle started out murdering her victims with poison, but this was sometimes a slow process. As she became more consumed by greed, she began to kill in more violent ways. Some victims were struck in the head with a meat cleaver; another was struck with a meat grinding machine. Her choice of weapons were interesting, as one would assume they were spur of the moment actions, given they were simple kitchen utensils and machines. But one thing for sure about Belle, she was calculating and planned her actions, so there was nothing spur of the moment about any of the murders.

Usually when a person uses a weapon to commit murder, there are underlying reasons behind it. Women generally stick to methods such as poisoning, because it's cleaner, or in some cases, a firearm. If Belle had used a firearm it would have ensured a quick death, but by striking them in the head it is almost as though she wanted to suffer as they died. While it's true that a direct blow to the head can sometimes be instantly fatal, there are plenty of other cases where the person has lingered before dying.

The use of a weapon is often seen in cases where there is rage, feelings of vengeance, and personal emotions tied up in the act itself. To strike a person is to 'hit out' at them. Sure there have been serial killers that used knives and other instruments to kill their victims, but they usually tortured or abused them to some degree beforehand. Belle most likely used violence to kill the adult males because she still harbored a lot of anger towards men because of what had happened to her when she was young.

It is uncertain what methods were used to kill the children, other than the last three to perish. They were allegedly poisoned, smothered with chloroform, and then left to burn in the fire. They were most likely dead before the fire was even lit, which in some ways, was probably a blessing, as it saved them from the terrifying suffering of burning to death.

While poisoning is often considered the less violent mode of murder, it can actually be a violent act for the victim. Most common poisons such as arsenic and strychnine cause excruciating abdominal pain for the victim. Some poison victims are known to absolutely writhe in pain shortly before their death. It has been suggested that Belle liked to use poison to mimic the pain she felt while going through the miscarriage. Losing a child can be physically painful, and it would be surprise if she wanted men to feel the pain that she had.

Sacrificing Children

Belle is certainly not the only woman to have murdered her own children, but there is a stark difference between those other women and Belle. Almost all cases of women killing their children are due to postpartum depression, or some other mental illness. Postpartum depression can range from the 'baby blues' through to psychosis and it is when it reaches the severity of psychosis that child murder can occur.

As far as is known, Belle had not suffered from postpartum depression, postpartum psychosis, or any other form of identified mental illness. This cruel, cold woman murdered her children for her own personal gain. In some cases there was a financial gain, such as with the deaths of her first two children who had been insured shortly before they died.

The killing of Jennie was most likely because she had witnessed one of the murders. The same goes for little Myrtle, who had told a classmate her mama had killed her daddy. Although it is unknown whether or not Belle knew of Myrtle's statement to her friend, it is assumed that she was worried Myrtle would tell the authorities, and her actions would be discovered.

It is more likely that the last three children were killed because they were a nuisance. If Belle was going to fake her own death and make a run for it, she could hardly drag three kids along with her. Not only would they slow her down, but it would also be more difficult to hide. Also, Belle may have feared that if she took them with her, the day may come where one of the children opened their mouths and told all.

The murder of the children also suited Belle's plan to set Ray Lamphere up for the murders and the fire. By making it look as though he had killed innocent children, she could be assured he would be hanged for the murders. This plan backfired though, as Ray was found innocent of all of the murders and was simply found guilty of the arson. The arson that he probably didn't even commit, but it was better than being found guilty of murder! One meant a prison sentence, the other meant death.

One has to wonder why Belle even had children, or fostered other people's children. She clearly had no empathy for anyone, so why would she have bothered? Unless she saw them as just a potential investment financially. By the time they had moved to the farm in La Porte, Belle had already had numerous claims and payouts from insurance companies from dead children, husbands, a business fire and several house fires. Perhaps she felt it was too risky to do the same with the remaining three children, considering she had already been investigated over the death of her husband Peter.

This meant the children were more or less useless to Belle. She had probably planned to kill them all along, but waited until the time was right.

CHAPTER 17:
Tombstones for the Victims

Many of Belle's victims were buried in Patton Cemetery and Pine Lake Cemetery, including both those that were identified and those who were unknown. Retired teacher Bruce Johnson, who is also an expert on Belle Gunness, decided that in 2008, the 100 year anniversary of the burning of Belle's house, he would help to place tombstones on the graves of the victims.

His reasoning for this was to preserve an important part of history for future generations to come. However, he at first was unable to locate the grave of who he considered to be Belle's last victim, Ray Lamphere. He was not buried in the same cemeteries as the other victims, as many felt that he was an accomplice not a victim. But Bruce Johnson saw it completely differently.

He believes that Ray thought he was setting himself up to be married to Belle and to co-own and manage the farm with her. He had a pretty sweet deal there, living in the house and working the farm alongside Belle. Ray had even fallen in love with large Norwegian woman. But all that was to change when Andrew Helgelien visited the farm.

Ray nicknamed Andrew the 'Big Swede' even though he was from Norway, and he saw him as a threat to his potential happiness with Belle. During the whole time Ray worked at the farm, Andrew was the only visitor that came. Ray became very jealous of Andrew, and this is most likely why Belle fired him. And that's when all the trouble started for Ray. Arrests, charges, and finally prison befell Ray, simply because he was unfortunate enough to become entangled with the dreadful Belle.

For this reason, Johnson felt that Ray also deserved to have a gravestone, so he set about trying to locate where he was buried. He spoke with one of Ray's descendants who believed him to be buried in the old Michigan City Jail Cemetery, but that had since been covered with building extensions.

Finally, the name of Rossburg Cemetery was brought into the picture. Sure enough, with some investigation, Johnson found that Ray had been buried there. The reason it had been so difficult to find the grave was because there was no headstone. Apparently it had been stolen and never recovered.

To finance a new headstone for Ray Lamphere's grave, Johnson used the proceeds he received from selling copies of a documentary he made with Stephen Ruminski, called 'The Gunness Mystery'. It seemed appropriate that the story of

Belle Gunness should eventually pay for a headstone for the man she tried to set up for the murder of herself and her children.

CHAPTER 18:
The Aftermath

With crimes such as those committed by Belle, those who were murdered were not the only victims. The effect was far more widespread, and with the mystery surrounding whether she had perished in the fire or not, leading to the effect lasting for decades. Most often following a murder, while the families are affected for a lifetime, other people tend to move forward after a year or so. But these murders at the hands of Belle were so cruel and so many, that memories of them would plague the citizens for 30 or more years.

Naturally, those who were most affected immediately were the family members and close friends of those that were murdered. This was further compounded by the fact that the majority of the victims were from Europe, particularly Norway, so the families often didn't even know what had happened to their relative – they had simply disappeared.

Murder comes in many shapes and forms, but to lose someone because of money, makes it all the more worse. It showed that Belle thought nothing of human life, that anyone was expendable if there was some sort of payday at the end of the day. To know that someone as cold and ruthless as Belle was the last person their loved one saw or spoke to was devastating to many people.

The true figure of how many people Belle murdered is unclear, but it is estimated to be around the 48 mark. When you consider that each of these people may have had parents, siblings, children, and other immediate family members, the number of those affected by the act of murder was tremendous. All of these people would never quite be the same again, because of Belle Gunness.

When suspicions arose that the body found in the burnt out house was not Belle, the people of La Porte lived in continuous fear. They looked over their shoulders all the time, to make sure Belle wasn't following them. Many wouldn't even venture out after dark, in case she was lurking in the shadows. Most who had known Belle thought quite highly of her, and she had friends among her neighbors. To suddenly learn that the person you thought you knew had done something so horrific was devastating to many. It changed the way people looked at each other, and damaged those wholesome values of trust and friendship.

The farmhand Joe Maxson and the neighbors that rushed to the scene once the fire was discovered were also deeply impacted by what they saw. Not only had they frantically tried to waken Belle and her children who they thought were sleeping, but they also saw firsthand the blackened and charred remains after the fire was put out. Those kinds of sights would upset anyone, and a lot of people have difficulty forgetting what they saw.

Of course one can't mention the impact on victims without mentioning Ray Lamphere. The poor, hardworking, lapdog that was infatuated with Belle and the dream that one day they would marry and live happily ever after. Instead, she framed him for her murder, and made sure everyone she came across as well as the authorities would look to him first as a suspect. Ray wasn't a bad man, and he ended up dying in prison because of Belle. He had no life after meeting her – no opportunity to find someone else and marry, no chance of having children, and certainly no future with Belle.

Mention must also be given to the volunteers, the neighbors, the police and the experts that were all involved with this case. Those that were given the task of digging up the grounds looking for human remains would have been terribly affected. Not a day would go by without them recalling the smell, the bones, the rotting flesh and the pigs.

And of course just when things were returning to some form of normalcy, along comes Esther Carlson, arrested for the murder of her employer. Her likeness to Belle, the similarities between them, and the suspicion that she was in fact Belle Gunness, would again bring all those memories back to those who had lived through the hell that was brought about by Belle Gunness.

Sadly, that mystery is yet to be solved, as there is still no definitive evidence to date that Esther and Belle were the same person. For many, it is irrefutable, and they are convinced they were one woman, even though there is no proof. The thought that she had been living all this time as another woman would have been not only terrifying, but infuriating, to many people, because she had literally gotten away with so many murders.

It must be considered though, that if Esther was not Belle, then what really happened to her? It's fairly clear that it wasn't her body found in the ruins of the farmhouse after the fire. Although she had amassed quite a fortune by then, Belle had been killing for money for so long, it is unlikely she would have been able to just stop. Once serial killers start killing, the only thing that stops them usually is death or imprisonment.

If Belle went on to live for quite some time after the fire, it would be almost certain that she killed again. But because nobody knows where she went, and there were no verified witness accounts, there is no way of knowing if she continued to kill or how. Perhaps she did leave the country; she certainly had the finances to do so. In which case, there could be other victims out there that have just not been linked to Belle.

CHAPTER 19:
Belle's Legacy and Media

A legend such as Belle, despite how evil she was, will always result in some sort of media, whether it is books, movies or music. Belle was certainly a popular topic in many!

Books

Lonely Heart – a short story written by Damon Runyon in 1937, about the Gunness case and Ray Lamphere.

The Bad Seed – A novel, film and Broadway play that have a character called Bessie Denker, who was based roughly on Belle Gunness. Written in 1954.

A House on the Plains – another short story about the Gunness case written by E.L. Doctorow.

Music

A folk song written in 1938 was about Belle Gunness.

Black Widow of La Porte – track from the album The Devil Knows My Name but John 5 in 2007.

Bella the Butcher – a song from the album Grim Scary Tales by Macabre is about Belle Gunness.

Radio Play

The Female Ogre – broadcast on a radio show called Nick Harris, Detective in 1940.

Film

Method – a movie inspired by the Gunness murders which was produced in 2004.

Belle Gunness – A Serial Killer From Selbu – a documentary made in 2005, directed by Anne Berit Vestby.

True Nightmares – an Investigation Discovery series had an episode called 'Crazy Love' and was a profile of Belle Gunness. It aired in 2015.

Brewery

Backroad Brewery – a La Porte microbrewery produces an Irish stout named after Belle.

The Conclusion

There are three remaining questions that are at the forefront of the mystery surrounding the apparent death of Belle Gunness:

- Did she really die in the fire?
- Who did the headless corpse belong to and where was the head?
- Did Belle assume the persona of Esther Carlson?

The answer to the first question, although unproven, must be no, she did not die in the fire. There were too many inconsistencies between the corpse that was found in the ruins, and Belle herself, and any evidence was purely circumstantial. Ray Lamphere, the many initially arrested for the murders of Belle and her children, didn't have it in him to kill. He certainly hadn't done so before, so why would he do it now? And for what reason would he kill her children?

If Belle was the body in the fire ruins, what would have been the point in removing her head and taking it away? Surely, even if she had been decapitated during the murder, the killer would have just left it there to burn along with the body. So, when considering the facts surrounding the possible motive behind the fire, and how the body was just too small, the only logical conclusion is that Belle had set up the whole thing herself and escaped.

While this theory explains the first question, it doesn't answer the second. If the body was not Belle, then who was the woman that was murdered and put in her place? The only clue really was that Belle had been seen the day before in the company of a younger woman who was a stranger to La Porte. We know that Belle killed for purpose, and clearly the purpose of this murder was to stage her own death, but how did she meet this woman and where did she come from?

Nobody has ever come forward and claimed a missing female friend or relative in that time in the surrounding area, Which suggests that this poor woman had come from further afield than La Porte. If Belle had been so successful in attracting men via newspaper advertisements, is it not plausible that she may have placed one looking for a housekeeper or a nanny for her children?

Belle had become an expert at luring men in and charming them out of their savings, so it is not a big stretch to think that she could have applied the same cunning in attracting a woman she could use for her getaway plan. Because Belle most certainly had a plan – she had already invoked suspicion about Ray Lamphere around town in the days leading up to the fire, written her will and cleaned out her bank account. Interesting how she made out her will leaving her money to an orphanage and then drew it all out!

Every detail regarding how she was going to stage her death and escape would have been thought of and put into place. Belle clearly was not a person of low intelligence. If she had been, she wouldn't have gotten away with the murders for such a long time. Plus she had taken on insurance companies and beaten them when they accused her of murdering her husband for money. Some people are born with academic intelligence, those that flourish at school and university, and others are born with a special kind of intelligence. The kind that enables them to manipulate and control the people around them. That kind of cunning is what helped Belle get away with multiple murders.

Finally, the question surrounding the possibility that Esther Carlson was actually Belle Gunness. Witnesses identified Esther as Belle after her death, but by then, Esther's secrets had been taken to her grave, so nobody really knew for sure. The resemblance between the two women was striking, and the manner and motive behind the murders they allegedly committed were almost identical. Could Belle have escaped to Arizona and assumed this woman's identity? Could the body in the fire have actually been Esther Carlson? If so, how did they meet?

When a story has so many mysteries attached to it, it is difficult to work out what is fact and what is fiction. There are always going to be rumors and theories when these things happen, and unfortunately, this can greatly affect whether or not a mystery is solved. The only way the true identity of the body in Belle's grave and the identity of Esther Carlson will ever be known, is if the researchers can find enough DNA to test it.

However, regardless of who these women really were, the facts about Belle Gunness and the murders must always be remembered for the sake of the victims. Around 48 people lost their lives at the hands of Belle, and this figure could even be higher. She poisoned, bludgeoned, hacked and buried men, women and children, without a second thought. Her thoughts were only of herself and what she could gain financially from the deaths of others.

FREE BONUS CHAPTER

The making of a serial killer

"I was born with the devil in me," said H.H. Holmes, who in 1893 took advantage of the World's Fair – and the extra room he rented out in his Chicago mansion – to kill at least 27 people without attracting much attention.

"I could not help the fact that I was a murderer, no more than the poet can help the inspiration to sing. I was born with the evil one standing as my sponsor beside the bed where I was ushered into the world, and he has been with me since," Holmes said.

The idea of "I can't help it" is one of the hallmarks of many serial killers, along with an unwillingness to accept responsibility for their actions and a refusal to acknowledge that they themselves used free will to do their dreadful deeds.

"Yes, I did it, but I'm a sick man and can't be judged by the standards of other men," said Juan Corona, who killed 25 migrant workers in California in the late 1960s and early 1970s, burying them in the very fruit orchards where they'd hoped to build a better life for their families.

Dennis Rader, who called himself the BTK Killer (Bind, Torture, Kill) also blamed some unknown facet to his personality, something he called Factor X, for his casual ability to kill one family, then go home to his own, where he was a devoted family man.

"When this monster entered my brain, I will never know, but it is here to stay. How does one cure himself? I can't stop it, the monster goes on, and hurts me as well as society. Maybe you can stop him. I can't," said Rader, who said he realized he was different than the other kids before he entered high school. "I actually think I may be possessed with demons."

But again, he blamed others for not stopping him from making his first murderous move.

"You know, at some point in time, someone should have picked something up from me and identified it," he later said.

Rader was not the only serial killer to place the blame far away from himself.

William Bonin actually took offense when a judge called him "sadistic and guilty of monstrous criminal conduct."

"I don't think he had any right to say that to me," Bonin later whined. "I couldn't help myself. It's not my fault I killed those boys."

It leaves us always asking why

For those of us who are not serial killers, the questions of why and how almost always come to mind, so ill equipped are we to understand the concept of murder on such a vast scale.

"Some nights I'd lie awake asking myself, 'Who the hell is this BTK?'" said FBI profiler John Douglas, who worked the Behavioral Science Unit at Quantico before writing several best-selling books, including "Mindhunter: Inside the FBI's Elite Serial Crime Unit," and "Obsession: The FBI's Legendary Profiler Probes the Psyches of Killers, Rapists, and Stalkers and Their Victims and Tells How to Fight Back."

The questions were never far from his mind - "What makes a guy like this do what he does? What makes him tick?" – and it's the kind of thing that keeps profilers and police up at night, worrying, wondering and waiting for answers that are not always so easily forthcoming.

Another leader into the study of madmen, the late FBI profiler Robert Ressler - who coined the terms serial killer as well as criminal profiling – also spent sleepless nights trying to piece together a portrait of many a killer, something that psychiatrist James Brussel did almost unfailingly well in 1940, when a pipe bomb killer enraged at Con Edison was terrorizing New York City.

(Brussel told police what the killer would be wearing when they arrested him, and although he was caught at home late at night, wearing his pajamas, when police asked him to dress, he emerged from his room wearing a double-breasted suit, exactly as Brussel had predicted.)

"What is this force that takes a hold of a person and pushes them over the edge?" wondered Ressler, who interviewed scores of killers over the course of his illustrious career.

In an effort to infiltrate the minds of serial killers, Douglas and Ressler embarked on a mission to interview some of the most deranged serial killers in the country, starting their journey in California, which "has always had more than its share of weird and spectacular crimes," Douglas said.

In their search for a pattern, they determined that there are essential two types of serial killers: organized and disorganized.

Organized killers

Organized killers were revealed through their crime scenes, which were neat, controlled and meticulous, with effort taken both in the crime and with their victims. Organized killers also take care to leave behind few clues once they're done.

Dean Corll was an organized serial killer. He tortured his victims overnight, carefully collecting blood and bodily fluids on a sheet of plastic before rolling them up and burying them and their possessions, most beneath the floor of a boat shed he'd rented, going there late at night under the cover of darkness.

Disorganized killers

On the flip side of the coin, disorganized killers grab their victims indiscriminately, or act on the spur of the moment, allowing victims to collect evidence beneath their fingernails when they fight back and oftentimes leaving behind numerous clues including weapons.

"The disorganized killer has no idea of, or interest in, the personalities of his victims," Ressler wrote in his book "Whoever Fights Monsters," one of several detailing his work as a criminal profiler. "He does not want to know who they are, and many times takes steps to obliterate their personalities by quickly knocking them unconscious or covering their faces or otherwise disfiguring them."

Cary Stayner – also known as the Yosemite Killer – became a disorganized killer during his last murder, which occurred on the fly when he was unable to resist a pretty park educator.

Lucky for other young women in the picturesque park, he left behind a wide range of clues, including four unmatched tire tracks from his aging 1979 International Scout.

"The crime scene is presumed to reflect the murderer's behavior and personality in much the same way as furnishings reveal the homeowner's character," Douglas and Ressler later wrote, expanding on their findings as they continued their interview sessions.

Serial killers think they're unique – but they're not

Dr. Helen Morrison – a longtime fixture in the study of serial killers who keeps clown killer John Wayne Gacy's brain in her basement (after Gacy's execution she sent the brain away for an analysis that proved it to be completely normal) – said that at their core, most serial killers are essentially the same.

While psychologists still haven't determined the motives behind what drives serial killers to murder, there are certain characteristics they have in common, said Morrison, who has studied or interviewed scores of serial killers and wrote about her experiences in "My Life Among the Serial Killers."

Most often men, serial killers tend to be talkative hypochondriacs who develop a remorseless addiction to the brutality of murder.

Too, they are able to see their victims as inanimate objects, playthings, of you will, around simply for their amusement.

Empathy? Not on your life.

"They have no appreciation for the absolute agony and terror and fear that the victim is demonstrating," said Morrison. "They just see the object in front of them. A serial murderer has no feelings. Serial killers have no motives. They kill only to kill an object."

In doing so, they satisfy their urges, and quiet the tumultuous turmoil inside of them.

"You say to yourself, 'How could anybody do this to another human being?'" Morrison said. "Then you realize they don't see them as humans. To them, it's like pulling the wings off a fly or the legs off a daddy longlegs.... You just want to see what happens. It's the most base experiment."

Nature vs. nurture?

For many serial killers, the desire to kill is as innate at their hair or eye color, and out of control, but most experts say that childhood trauma is an experience shared by them all.

In 1990, Colin Wilson and Donald Seaman conducted a study of serial killers behind bars and found that childhood problems were the most influential factors that led serial killers down their particular path of death and destruction.

Former FBI profiler Robert Ressler – who coined the terms serial killer and criminal profiling – goes so far as to say that 100 percent of all serial killers experienced childhoods that were not filled with happy memories of camping trips or fishing on the lake.

According to Ressler, of all the serial killers he interviewed or studied, each had suffered some form of abuse as a child -

either sexual, physical or emotional abuse, neglect or rejection by parents or humiliation, including instances that occurred at school.

For those who are already hovering psychologically on edge due to unfortunate genetics, such events become focal points that drive a killer to act on seemingly insane instincts.

Because there is often no solid family unit – parents are missing or more focused on drugs and alcohol, sexual abuse goes unnoticed, physical abuse is commonplace – the child's development becomes stunted, and they can either develop deep-seeded rage or create for themselves a fantasy world where everything is perfect, and they are essentially the kings of their self-made castle.

That was the world of Jeffrey Dahmer, who recognized his need for control much later, after hours spent in analysis where he learned the impact of a sexual assault as a child as well as his parents' messy, rage-filled divorce.

"After I left the home, that's when I started wanting to create my own little world, where I was the one who had complete control," Dahmer said. "I just took it way too far."

Dahmer's experiences suggest that psychopathic behavior likely develops in childhood, when due to neglect and abuse, children revert to a place of fantasy, a world where the victimization of the child shifts toward others.

"The child becomes sociopathic because the normal development of the concepts of right and wrong and empathy towards others is retarded because the child's emotional and social development occurs within his self-centered fantasies. A person can do no wrong in his own world and the pain of others is of no consequence when the purpose of the fantasy world is to satisfy the needs of one person," according to one expert.

As the lines between fantasy and reality become blurred, fantasies that on their own are harmless become real, and monsters like Dean Corll find themselves strapping young boys down to a wooden board, raping them, torturing them and listening to them scream, treating the act like little more than a dissociative art project that ends in murder.

Going inside the mind: Psychopathy and other mental illnesses

While not all psychopaths are serial killers – many compulsive killers do feel some sense of remorse, such as Green River Killer Gary Ridgeway did when he cried in court after one victim's father offered Ridgeway his forgiveness – those who are, Morrison said, are unable to feel a speck of empathy for their victims.

Their focus is entirely on themselves and the power they are able to assert over others, especially so in the case of a psychopath.

Psychopaths are charming – think Ted Bundy, who had no trouble luring young women into his car by eliciting sympathy with a faked injury – and have the skills to easily manipulate their victims, or in some cases, their accomplices.

Dean Corll was called a Svengali – a name taken from a fictional character in George du Maurier's 1895 novel "Trilby" who seduces, dominates and exploits the main character, a young girl – for being able to enlist the help of several neighborhood boys who procured his youthful male victims without remorse, even when the teens were their friends.

Some specific traits of serial killers, determined through years of profiling, include:

- **Smooth talking but insincere.** Ted Bundy was a charmer, the kind of guy that made it easy for people to be swept into his web. "I liked him immediately, but people like Ted can fool you completely," said Ann Rule, author of the best-selling "Stranger Beside Me," about her experiences with Bundy, a man she considered a friend. "I'd been a cop, had all that psychology — but his mask was perfect. I say that long acquaintance can help you know someone. But you can never be really sure. Scary."

- **Egocentric and grandiose.** Jack the Ripper thought the world of himself, and felt he would outsmart police, so much so that he sent letters taunting the London officers. "Dear Boss," he wrote, "I keep on hearing the police have caught me but they won't fix me just yet. I have laughed when they look so clever and talk about being on the right track. That joke about Leather Apron gave me real fits. I am down on whores and I shan't quit ripping them till I do get buckled. Grand work the last job was. I gave the lady no time to squeal. How can they catch me now? I love my work and want to start again. You will soon hear of me with my funny little games. I saved some of the proper red stuff in a ginger beer bottle over the last job to write with but it went thick like glue and I can't use it. Red ink is fit enough I hope ha. ha. The next job I do I shall clip the lady's ears off and send to the police officers … My knife's so nice and sharp I want to get to work right away if I get a chance. Good luck."

- **Lack of remorse or guilt.** Joel Rifkin was filled with self-pity after he was convicted of killing and dismembering at least nine women. He called his conviction a tragedy, but later, in prison, he got into an argument with mass murderer Colin Ferguson over whose killing spree was more important, and when Ferguson taunted him for only killing women, Rifkin said, "Yeah, but I had more victims."

- **Lack of empathy.** Andrei Chikatilo, who feasted on bits of genitalia both male and female after his kills, thought nothing of taking a life, no matter how torturous it was for his victims. "The whole thing - the cries, the blood, the agony - gave me relaxation and a certain pleasure," he said.

- **Deceitful and manipulative.** John Wayne Gacy refused to take responsibility for the 28 boys buried beneath his house, even though he also once said that clowns can get away with murder. "I think after 14 years under truth serum had I committed the crime I would have known it," said the man the neighbors all claimed to like. "There's got to be something that would... would click in my mind. I've had photos of 21 of the victims and I've looked at them all over the years here and I've never recognized anyone of them."

- **Shallow emotions.** German serial killer Rudolph Pliel, convicted of killing 10 people and later took his own life in prison, compared his "hobby" of murder to playing cards, and later told police, "What I did is not such a great harm, with all these surplus women nowadays. Anyway, I had a good time."

- **Impulsive.** Tommy Lynn Sells, who claimed responsibility for dozens of murders throughout the Midwest and South, saw a woman at a convenience store and followed her home, an impulse he was unable to control. He waited until the house went dark, then "I went into this house. I go to the first bedroom I see...I don't know whose room it is and, and, and, and I start stabbing." The victim was the woman's young son.

- **Poor behavior controls**. "I wished I could stop but I could not. I had no other thrill or happiness," said UK killer Dennis Nilsen, who killed at least 12 young men via strangulation, then bathed and dressed their bodies before disposing of them, often by burning them.

- **Need for excitement.** For Albert Fish - a masochistic killer with a side of sadism that included sending a letter to the mother of one of his victims, describing in detail how he cut, cooked and ate her daughter - even the idea of his own death was one he found particularly thrilling. "Going to the electric chair will be the supreme thrill of my life," he said.

- **Lack of responsibility.** "I see myself more as a victim rather than a perpetrator," said Gacy, in a rare moment of admitting the murders. "I was cheated out of my childhood. I should never have been convicted of anything more serious than running a cemetery without a license. They were just a bunch of worthless little queers and punks."

- **Early behavior problems.** "When I was a boy I never had a friend in the world," said German serial killer Heinrich Pommerencke, who began raping and murdering girls as a teen.

- **Adult antisocial behavior.** Gary Ridgeway pleaded guilty to killing 48 women, mostly prostitutes, who were easy prey and were rarely reported missing – at least not immediately. "I don't believe in man, God nor Devil. I hate the whole damned human race, including myself... I preyed upon the weak, the harmless and the unsuspecting. This lesson I was taught by others: Might makes right."

'I felt like it'

Many psychopaths will say after a crime, "I did it because I felt like it," with a certain element of pride.

That's how BTK killer Dennis Rader felt, and because he had no sense of wrong regarding his actions, he was able to carry on with his normal life with his wife and children with ease.

Someone else's demeanor might have changed, they may have become jittery or anxious, and they would have been caught.

Many serial killers are so cold they are can pop into a diner right after a murder, never showing a sign of what they've done.

"Serial murderers often seem normal," according to the FBI. "They have families and/or a steady job."

"They're so completely ordinary," Morrison added. "That's · what gets a lot of victims in trouble."

That normalcy is often what allows perpetrators to get away with their crimes for so long.

Unlike mass murderers such as terrorists who generally drop off the radar before perpetrating their event, serial killers blend in. They might seem a bit strange – neighbors noticed that Ed Gein wasn't too big on personal hygiene, and neighbors did think it was odd that William Bonin hung out with such young boys - but not so much so that anyone would ask too many questions.

"That's why so many people often say, "I had no idea" or "He was such a nice guy" after a friend or neighbor is arrested.

And it's also why people are so very, very stunned when they see stories of serial killers dominating the news.

"For a person with a conscience, Rader's crimes seem hideous, but from his point of view, these are his greatest accomplishments and he is anxious to share all of the wonderful things he has done," said Jack Levin, PhD, director of the Brudnick Center on Violence and Conflict at Northeastern University in Boston and the author of "Extreme Killings."

A new take on psychopathy

Psychopathy is now diagnosed as antisocial personality disorder, a prettier spin on an absolutely horrifying diagnosis.

According to studies, almost 50 percent of men in prison and 21 percent of women in prison have been diagnosed with antisocial personality disorder.

Of serial killers, Ted Bundy (who enjoyed sex with his dead victims), John Wayne Gacy and Charles Manson (who encouraged others to do his dirty work which included the murder of pregnant Sharon Tate) were all diagnosed with this particular affliction, which allowed them to carry out their crimes with total disregard toward others or toward the law.

They showed no remorse.

Schizophrenia

Many known serial killers were later diagnosed with some other form of mental illness, including schizophrenia, believed to be behind the crimes of David Berkowitz (he said his neighbor's dog told him to kill his six victims in the 1970s), Ed Gein, whose grisly saving of skin, bones and various female sex parts was a desperate effort to resurrect his death mother and Richard Chase (the vampire of Sacramento, who killed six people in California in order to drink their blood).

Schizophrenia includes a wide range of symptoms, ranging from hallucinations and delusions to living in a catatonic state.

Borderline personality disorder

Borderline personality disorder – which is characterized by intense mood swings, problems with interpersonal relationships and impulsive behaviors – is also common in serial killers.

Some diagnosed cases of borderline personality disorder include Aileen Wuornos, a woman whose horrific childhood and numerous sexual assaults led her to murder one of her rapists, after which she spiraled out of control and killed six other men who picked her up along with highway in Florida, nurse Kristen H. Gilbert, who killed four patients at a Virginia hospital with overdoses of epinephrine, and Dahmer, whose murder count rose to 17 before he was caught.

With a stigma still quite present regarding mental illness, it's likely we will continue to diagnose serial killers and mass murderers after the fact, too late to protect their victims.

Top signs of a serial killer

While there is still no simple thread of similarities – which is why police and the FBI have more trouble in real life solving crimes than they do on shows like "Criminal Minds" – there are some things to look for, experts say.

- **Antisocial Behavior.** Psychopaths tend to be loners, so if a child that was once gregarious and outgoing becomes shy and antisocial, this could be an issue.

Jeffrey Dahmer was a social, lively child until his parents moved to Ohio for his father's new job. There, he regressed – allegedly after being sexually molested – and began focusing his attentions on dissecting road kill rather than developing friendships.

- **Arson.** Fire is power, and power and control are part of the appeal for serial killers, who enjoy having their victims at their mercy. David Berkowitz was a pyromaniac as a child – his classmates called him Pyro as a nickname, so well-known was he for his fire obsession - and he reportedly started more than 1,000 fires in New York before he became the Son of Sam killer.

- **Torturing animals.** Serial killers often start young, and test boundaries with animals including family or neighborhood pets. According to studies, 70 percent of violent offenders have episodes of animal abuse in their childhood histories, compared to just 6 percent of nonviolent offenders. Albert DeSalvo – better known as the Boston Strangler – would capture cats and dogs as a child and trap them in boxes, shooting arrows at the defenseless animals for sport.

- **A troubled family history.** Many serial killers come from families with criminal or psychiatric histories or alcoholism. Edmund Kemper killed his grandparents to see what it would be like, and later – after he murdered a string of college students – he killed his alcoholic mother, grinding her vocal chords in the garbage disposal in an attempt to erase the sound of her voice.

- **Childhood abuse.** William Bonin – who killed at least 21 boys and young men in violent rapes and murders – was abandoned as a child, sent to live in a group home where he himself was sexually assaulted. The connections suggest either a rage that can't be erased – Aileen Wuornos, a rare female serial killer, was physically and sexually abused throughout her childhood, resulting in distrust of others and a pent-up rage that exploded during a later rape - or a disassociation of sorts, refusing to connect on a human level with others for fear of being rejected yet again.

- **Substance abuse.** Many serial killers use drugs or alcohol. Jeffrey Dahmer was discharged from the Army due to a drinking problem he developed in high school, and he used alcohol to lure his victims to his apartment, where he killed them in a fruitless effort to create a zombie-like sex slave who would never leave him.

- **Voyeurism.** When Ted Bundy was a teen, he spent his nights as a Peeping Tom, hoping to get a glimpse of one of the neighborhood girls getting undressed in their bedrooms.

- **Serial killers are usually smart.** While their IQ is not usually the reason why serial killers elude police for so long, many have very high IQs. Edmund Kemper was thisclose to being considered a genius (his IQ was 136, just four points beneath the 140 mark that earns genius status), and he used his intelligence to create complex cons that got him released from prison early after killing his grandparents, allowing eight more women to die.

- **Can't keep a job.** Serial killers often have trouble staying employed, either because their off-hours activities take up a lot of time (Jeffrey Dahmer hid bodies in his shower, the shower he used every morning before work, because he was killing at such a fast rate) or because their obsessions have them hunting for victims when they should be on the clock.

Trademarks of a serial killer

While what we know helps us get a better understanding of potential serial killers – and perhaps take a closer look at our weird little neighbors – it is still tricky for police and FBI agents to track serial killers down without knowing a few tells.

The signature

While serial killers like to stake a claim over their killings – "Serial killers typically have some sort of a signature," according to Dr. Scott Bonn, a professor at Drew University in New Jersey – they are usually still quite neat, and a signature does not necessarily mean evidence.

"Jack the Ripper, of course, his signature was the ripping of the bodies," said Bonn.

While there are multiple theories, Jack the Ripper has yet to be identified, despite the similarities in his murders.

Too, the Happy Face Killer, Keith Hunter Jespersen – whose childhood was marked by alcoholic parents, teasing at school and a propensity to abuse small animals - drew happy faces on the numerous letters he sent to both media and authorities, teasing them a bit with a carrot on a string.

"If the forensic evidence itself - depending upon the bones or flesh or whatever is left - if it allows for that sort of identification, that would be one way of using forensic evidence to link these murders," Bonn said.

The cooling off period

Organized killers are so neat, tidy and meticulous that they may never leave clues, even if they have a signature.

And if there's a long cooling off period between crimes, tracking the killer becomes even more of a challenge.

After a murder – which could be compared to a sexual experience or getting high on drugs – the uncontrollable urges that led the killer to act dissipate, at least temporarily.

But according to Ressler, serial killers are rarely satisfied with their kills, and each one increases desire – in the same way a porn addiction can start with the pages of Playboy then turn into BDSM videos or other fetishes when Playboy pictorials are no longer satisfying.

"I was literally singing to myself on my way home, after the killing. The tension, the desire to kill a woman had built up in such explosive proportions that when I finally pulled the trigger, all the pressures, all the tensions, all the hatred, had just vanished, dissipated, but only for a short time," said David Berkowitz, better known as the Son of Sam.

Afterwards, the memory of the murder, or mementos from the murder such as the skulls Jeffrey Dahmer retained, the scalps collected by David Gore or the box of vulvas Ed Gein kept in his kitchen, no longer become enough, and the killers must kill again, creating a "serial" cycle.

That window between crimes usually becomes smaller, however, which allows authorities to notice similarities in murder scenes or methodology, making tracking easier.

In the case of William Bonin, there were months between his first few murders, but toward the end, he sometimes killed two young men a day to satisfy his increasingly uncontrollable urges.

"Sometimes... I'd get tense and think I was gonna go crazy if I couldn't get some release, like my head would explode. So I'd go out hunting. Killing helped me... It was like ... needing to go gambling or getting drunk. I had to do it," Bonin said.

Hunting in pairs

Some serial killers – between 10 and 25 percent - find working as a team more efficient, and they use their charm as the hook to lure in accomplices.

Ed Gein may never have killed anyone had his accomplice, a mentally challenged man who helped Gein dig up the graves of women who resembled his mother, not been sent to a nursing home, leaving Gein unable to dig up the dead on his own.

Texas killer Dean Corll used beer, drugs, money and candy to bribe neighborhood boys to bring him their friends for what they were promised was a party, but instead would turn to torture and murder. He would have killed many more if one of his accomplices had not finally shot him to prevent another night of death.

William Bonin also liked to work with friends, and he enticed boys who were reportedly on the low end of the IQ scale to help him sadistically rape and torture his victims.

Other red flags

According to the FBI's Behavioral Science Unit – founded by Robert Ressler - 60 percent of murderers whose crimes involved sex were childhood bed wetters, and sometimes carried the habit into adulthood. One such serial killer, Alton Coleman, regularly wet his pants, earning the humiliating nickname "Pissy."

Sexual arousal over violent fantasies during puberty can also play a role in a serial killer's future.

Jeffrey Dahmer hit puberty about the same time he was dissecting road kill, so in some way, his wires became crossed and twisted, and sex and death aroused him.

Brain damage? Maybe

While Helen Morrison's test found that John Wayne Gacy's brain was normal, and Jeffrey Dahmer's father never had the opportunity to have his son's brain studied, although both he and Jeffrey had wanted the study, there is some evidence that some serial killers have brain damage that impact their ability to exact rational control.

"Normal parents? Normal brains? I think not," said Dr. Jonathan Pincus, a neurologist and author of the book "Base Instincts: What Makes Killers Kill."

"Abusive experiences, mental illnesses and neurological deficits interplayed to produce the tragedies reported in the newspapers. The most vicious criminals have also been, overwhelmingly, people who have been grotesquely abused as children and have paranoid patterns of thinking," said Pincus in his book, adding that childhood traumas can impact the developmental anatomy and functioning of the brain.

***

So what do we know?

Serial killers can be either uber-smart or brain damaged, completely people savvy or totally awkward, high functioning and seemingly normal or unable to hold down a job.

But essentially, no matter what their back story, their modus operandi or their style, "they're evil," said criminal profiler Pat Brown.

And do we need to know anything more than that?

More books by Jack Rosewood

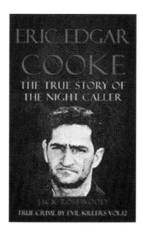

The Night Caller, The Nedlands Monster, and Eric Edgar Cooke, are the names used to describe one of the most brutal serial killers in Australian History. Over the space of 5 years, he not only murdered 8 people, he also attempted to murder 14 others, because he just wanted to hurt people. Was he crazy?

Nobody was safe from Eric Edgar Cooke. He was an opportunistic killer, selecting victims randomly. Whoever crossed his path during those hot humid nights would fall victim to his variety of killing methods. You were not safe in your homes, or walking down the road at night.

This serial killer biography will delve into the life and eventual execution of Eric Edgar Cooke, the last man hanged for murder in Perth, Western Australia. The deeds of Eric Edgar Cooke created fear and horror in the people of Perth. The true accounts from the survivors will show you how they lived through this Australian true crime.

If you are a lover of serial killers true crime, you will be enthralled by this investigative book. You will discover how it is that he could get away with his crimes for so long. Why is it that the detectives thought he was just a likeable rogue and petty thief? Discover how one man could change the lives of an entire town and become a bogeyman character for decades after his death. True crime murder doesn't get more complexing or bewildering as the story of Eric Edgar Cooke.

During fifty one days in early 1993 one of the most tragic events in American crime history unfolded on the plains outside Waco, Texas. An obscure and heavily armed religious sect called the Branch Davidians was barricaded inside their commune and outside were hundreds of law enforcement angry because the former had killed four ATF agents in a botched raid. Open the pages of this book and go on an engaging and captivating ride to examine one of the most important true crime stories in recent decades. Read the shocking true story of how a man the government considered a psychopath, but whose followers believed to be a prophet, led a breakaway sect of the Seventh Day Adventist Church into infamy.

You will follow the meteoric rise of the Branch Davidians' charismatic leader, David Koresh, as he went from an awkward kid in remedial classes to one of the most infamous cult leaders in world history. But the story of the Waco Siege begins long before the events of 1993. At the core of the conflict between the Branch Davidians and the United States government were ideas and interpretations of religious freedom and gun ownership, which as will be revealed in the pages of this book, a considerable philosophical gulf existed between the two sides. David Koresh and the Branch Davidians carried on a long tradition in American and Texas history of religious dissent, but in 1993 that dissent turned tragically violent.

You will find that beyond the standard media portrayals of the Waco Siege was an event comprised of complex human characters on both sides of the firing line and that perhaps the most tragic aspect of the event was that the extreme bloodshed could have been avoided.

The pages of this book will make you angry, sad, and bewildered; but no matter the emotions evoke, you will be truly moved by the events of the Waco Siege.

When Killing Cousins David Alan Gore and Fred Waterfield realized as teens that they shared the same sick, twisted sex fantasies of raping helpless, bound women who were completely at their mercy, Florida's quiet Vero Beach would be never be the same.

Some of the least remorseful of all American serial killers, the deadly duo stalked their victims, often hitchhikes they believed would never be missed, using Gore's auxiliary deputy badge as a ruse to lure them into their vehicle. After that, they were most likely to be driven to their deaths.

Their evil, sadistic story from the annals of Florida history is one that will chill even longtime fans of true crime murder, especially after reading excerpts from the letters Gore wrote from prison, in which he shared deplorable secrets that made him one of the most demented sex criminals of all time.

Gore once told a psychologist that "the devil made me do it," but those who came in contact with Gore – including the law enforcement officials that ultimately put him on Death Row – believed he was the devil due to his depraved levels of cruelty.

Among the psychopaths and sociopaths that have walked the earth, Gore was one of the worst, although those who knew them say that it was Fred Waterfield, the more popular cousin who always played the good guy to Gore's bad, who was the true brains of the outfit. As it happens, he probably was, because Waterfield almost got away with murder.

GET THE BOOK ABOUT HERBERT MULLIN FOR FREE

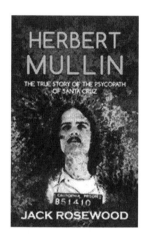

Go to <u>www.jackrosewood.com</u>

and get this E-Book for free!

A Note From The Author

Hello, this is Jack Rosewood. Thank you for reading this book. I hope you enjoyed the read of this chilling story. If you did, I'd appreciate if you would take a few moments to post a review on Amazon.

Here's the link to the book: Amazon

I would also love if you'd sign up to my newsletter to receive updates on new releases, promotions and a FREE copy of my Herbert Mullin E-Book at www.jackrosewood.com

Thanks again for reading this book, make sure to follow me on Facebook at Jack Rosewood author.

A big thanks to Rebecca Lo who co-wrote this book with me.

Best Regards

Jack Rosewood

Made in the USA
Lexington, KY
29 August 2018